To Gran,
Merry Christmas
1985

with much love,

Chris, Jim,
Caleb & Jacob

Poetry fills needs that cannot be met by any other form of writing. Thoughts that could fill a whole book are condensed into one or two sparkling sentences ...feelings that defy everyday expressions are illuminated by a word or phrase ... inspiration sweeps suddenly into the heart. Discover the world of great religious verse for yourself through the pages of

Best-Loved RELIGIOUS POEMS

" ... The reader will find much that will cheer and inspire in this collection...."

Moody Monthy

"Will delight one for general reading and as a sourcebook that will render service and real profit."

Presbyterian Life

By the Same Author

THE WORLD'S BEST LOVED POEMS
GREATEST THOUGHTS ABOUT GOD
GREATEST THOUGHTS ABOUT CHRIST
GREATEST THOUGHTS ABOUT THE BIBLE
THE WORLD'S BEST RELIGIOUS QUOTATIONS
CYCLOPEDIA OF RELIGIOUS ANECDOTES
DEEPER EXPERIENCES OF FAMOUS CHRISTIANS
THE MARKED BIBLE (MARKINGS)
THE PRECIOUS PROMISE BIBLE (MARKINGS)

THE BEST LOVED
RELIGIOUS POEMS

GLEANED FROM MANY SOURCES

BY

JAMES GILCHRIST LAWSON

FLEMING H. REVELL COMPANY
OLD TAPPAN, NEW JERSEY

ISBN   0-8007-0019-8

Copyright, 1933,
renewed 1961
FLEMING H. REVELL COMPANY

INTRODUCTION

THE compiler and publishers of this volume have tried to include in this collection all of the most popular Christian religious poems, and they believe that they have succeeded in doing so. This is probably the most complete anthology of favorite Christian poems yet offered to the public.

The poems herein were selected not because of literary merit from a critical standpoint, but because of their popularity and heart appeal. Most of them are of a deeply devotional character. Many of them would rank high judged strictly by literary standards. All rank high because of the great thoughts that they contain, and because they express these thoughts in a way which has gripped the hearts of the masses and which has made them popular.

The compiler has gleaned these poems from every possible source, but especially from the leading religious papers of which he has been a constant reader for many years. While editing several hundred monthly church magazines, during the last seven years, he has had the assistance of the pastors of prominent churches of Chicago and other cities in selecting the best religious poems for publication in their church magazines; and he is deeply grateful to these pastors for the help which they have given indirectly in the compiling of this book.

The compiler and publishers appreciate the coöperation that authors and publishers have given in allowing the use of their poems in this collection. The compiler has endeavored not to use any copyright poem without the consent of the owner, and so far as possible the consent of all living authors has been obtained for the use of their poems in this anthology.

Believing that this volume will be a great help in deepening the spiritual life and character of its readers, the compiler and publishers consign it to the public.

J. G. L.

Chicago, Illinois.

5

CONTENTS

8 CONTENTS

THE ATONEMENT

The Cross

The Cross is such a simple thing,
Yet of it men may talk and sing.

It is a ladder to the skies,
On which a mounting soul may rise.

It is a sign-board on the road,
To cheer man with his weary load.

It is a key that fits the door
To joyousness forever more.

It signals to the human race
That God in mercy offers grace.

To some it is a stumbling block
That causes men to curse and mock;

To others who their sins bemoan
It can become a stepping stone.

To voyagers its sturdy form
Becomes an anchor in the storm.

A hammer, it has won renown
By battering old oppressions down.

Gripped by still others as a sword,
It has won battles for the Lord.

Dragged as a plowshare thro' the heart,
New furrows cause the grain to start.

It is a tree upon a hill,
Whose fruit the hungry heart can fill.

It is a window for the soul;
'Tis medicine to make one whole.

The Cross is such a simple thing,
And yet it touches everything.

We cannot feel that such a sign
Is other than a power divine.

It is a beacon ever lit
By One identified with it.

—Charles N. Pace, D.D.

(Used by permission)

There Is a Green Hill Far Away

There is a green hill far away,
    Without a city wall,
Where the dear Lord was crucified,
    Who died to save us all.

CHORUS

Oh dearly, dearly has he loved,
    And we must love him too,
And trust in his redeeming blood,
    And try his works to do.

We may not know, we cannot tell,
    What pains he had to bear;
But we believe it was for us
    He hung and suffered there.

He died that we might be forgiven,
    He died to make us good,
That we might go at last to heaven,
    Saved by his precious blood.

There was no other good enough
    To pay the price of sin;
He only could unlock the gate
    Of heaven and let us in.

—Cecil Frances Alexander

THE BIBLE

Holy Bible, Book Divine

Holy Bible, book divine,
Precious treasure, thou art mine;
Mine to tell me whence I came;
Mine to teach me what I am.

Mine to chide me when I rove,
Mine to show a Saviour's love;
Mine art thou to guide my feet,
Mine to judge, condemn, acquit.

Mine to comfort in distress,
If the Holy Spirit bless;
Mine to show by living faith
Man can triumph over death.

Mine to tell of joys to come,
And the rebel sinner's doom;
Holy Bible, book divine,
Precious treasure, thou art mine.
                              —*John Burton*

O How Sweet Are Thy Words!

Father of mercies, in Thy Word
    What endless glory shines!
For ever be Thy Name adored
    For these celestial lines.

Here may the blind and hungry come,
    And light and food receive;
Here shall the lowliest guest have room,
    And taste and see and live.

Here springs of consolation rise
    To cheer the fainting mind;
And thirsty souls receive supplies,
    And sweet refreshment find.

Here the Redeemer's welcome voice
Spreads Heavenly peace around;
And life and everlasting joys
Attend the blissful sound.

O may these Heavenly pages be
My ever dear delight!
And still new beauties may I see,
And still increasing light!

Divine Instructor, Gracious Lord,
Be Thou forever near;
Teach me to love Thy Sacred Word
And view my Savior here.

—*Anne Steele*

The Bible

Within that awful volume lies
The mystery of mysteries.
Happiest they of human race
To whom their God has given grace
To read, to fear, to hope, to pray,
To lift the latch, and force the way;
And better had they ne'er been born
Who read to doubt, or read to scorn.

—*Walter Scott*

My Mother's Bible

This book is all that's left me now,
Tears will unbidden start—
With faltering lip and throbbing brow
I press it to my heart.
For many generations past,
Here is our family tree;
My mother's hand this Bible clasped;
She, dying, gave it me.

Ah! well do I remember those
  Whose names these records bear,
Who 'round the hearthstone used to close
  After the evening prayer,
And speak of what these pages said,
  In tones my heart would thrill!
Though they are with the silent dead
  Here are they living still!

My father read this holy book
  To brothers, sisters, dear;
How calm was my poor mother's look,
  Who loved God's word to hear
Her angel face—I see it yet!
  What thronging memories come!
Again that little group is met
  Within the halls of home!

Thou truest friend man ever knew,
  Thy constancy I've tried;
Where all were false, I found thee true,
  My counselor and guide.
The mines of earth no treasure give
  That could this volume buy;
In teaching me the way to live,
  It taught me how to die.
                              —*George P. Morris*

Just One Book

When Sir Walter Scott was dying, he asked Lockhart to read to him. "What book?" asked Lockhart. "What book?" cried Sir Walter. "There is but one Book—the Bible."

"There's just one Book!" cried the dying sage;
  "Read me the old, old story."
And the winged words that can never age
  Wafted him home to glory.
    There's just one Book.

There's just one Book for the tender years—
One Book alone for guiding
The little feet through the joys and fears
That unknown days are hiding.
    There's just one Book.

There's just one Book for the bridal hour,
One Book of love's own coining;
Its truths alone lend beauty and power
To vows that lives are joining.
    There's just one Book.

There's just one Book for life's gladness,
One Book for the toilsome days;
One Book that can cure life's madness;
One Book that can voice life's praise.
    There's just one Book.

There's just one Book for the dying,
One Book for the starting tears,
And one for the soul that's flying
Home for the measureless years.
    There's just one Book.

—Anonymous

The Anvil of God's Word

Last eve I paused beside the blacksmith's door,
    And heard the anvil ring the vesper chime;
Then looking in, I saw upon the floor,
    Old hammers worn with beating years of time.

"How many anvils have you had," said I,
    "To wear and batter all these hammers so?"
"Just one," said he, and then with twinkling eye,
    "The anvil wears the hammers out, you know."

"And so," I thought, "The Anvil of God's Word
    For ages sceptic blows have beat upon,
Yet, though the noise of falling blows was heard,
    The Anvil is unharmed, the hammers *gone*."

—John Clifford, D.D.

God's Precepts Perfect

The law of Jehovah is perfect, restoring the soul;
The testimony of Jehovah is sure, making wise the simple.
The precepts of Jehovah are right, rejoicing the heart;
The commandment of Jehovah is pure, enlightening the
   eyes.
The fear of Jehovah is clean, enduring forever;
The ordinances of Jehovah are true, and righteous alto-
   gether.

—Psalm 19:7-9

The Word of God

"The word of our God shall stand forever."—Isa. 40:8.

Though heart grows faint and spirits sink,
   By every wind of feeling blown;
Though faith itself may seem to fail,
   I rest upon Thy word alone,

That word of power that framed the worlds,
   Unfailing, changeless, strong, and sure.
Though heaven and earth should pass away,
   What Thou hast spoken must endure.

Is Thine arm shortened, Thine ear dulled?
   What Thou hast sworn hast Thou forgot?
God of the everlasting years,
   All else may fail; Thou failest not.

Against the foeman's fiery darts
   I wield anew the Spirit's sword,
And answer every fresh assault
   With ever-fresh "Thus saith the Lord."

And, when some promised blessing seems
   Too great, too wonderful for me,
I dare by faith to call it mine,
   With "It is written" all my plea.

'Mid shifting sands of doubt and fear
This is the one foundation-stone;
My soul hath cast her anchor here;
I rest upon Thy word alone.

—*Annie Johnson Flint*
(Used by permission)

My Old Bible

Though the cover is worn,
And the pages are torn,
    And though places bear traces of tears,
Yet more precious than gold
Is this Book worn and old,
    That can shatter and scatter my fears.

This old Book is my guide,
'Tis a friend by my side,
    It will lighten and brighten my way;
And each promise I find
Soothes and gladdens the mind,
    As I read it and heed it each day.

To this Book I will cling,
Of its worth I will sing,
    Though great losses and crosses be mine;
For I cannot despair,
Though surrounded by care,
    While possessing this blessing Divine.

—*Anonymous*

The Book Our Mothers Read

We search the world for truth; we cull
The good, the pure, the beautiful,
From graven stone and written scroll,
From all old flower-fields of the soul;

And, weary seekers of the best,
We come back laden from the quest,
To find that all the sages said
Is in the Book our mothers read.
                    —*John Greenleaf Whittier*

The Best of All

Blessed Bible, sacred treasure,
    Precious book, of all the best,
There is comfort never failing,
    And a calm abiding rest.
Read with reverence, and commit it,
    Verse by verse, and day by day;
'Tis the word that God has spoken,
    And it cannot pass away.
                    —*Fanny Crosby*

The Spirit's Light

The Spirit breathes upon the Word,
    And brings the truth to sight;
Precepts and promises afford
    A sanctifying light.

A glory gilds the sacred page
    Majestic like the sun;
It gives a light to every age—
    It gives, but borrows none.
                    —*Wm. Cowper*

BROTHERHOOD

All One In Christ

In Christ there is no east nor west,
  In him no south nor north,
But one great fellowship of love
  Throughout the whole wide earth.
In him shall true hearts everywhere
  Their high communion find—
His service is the golden cord
  Close-binding all mankind.

Join hands, then, brothers of the faith,
  Whate'er your race may be!
Who serves my Father as a son
  Is surely kin to me.
In Christ now meet both east and west,
  In him meet south and north,
All Christly souls are one in him
  Throughout the whole wide earth.

—*John Oxenham*

CHRIST

Credo

Not what, but Whom, I do believe,
That, in my darkest hour of need,
Hath comfort that no mortal creed
  To mortal man may give;—
Not what, but Whom!
For Christ is more than all the creeds,
And His full life of gentle deeds
  Shall all the creeds outlive.

Not what I do believe, but Whom!
Who walks beside me in the gloom?
Who shares the burden wearisome?
Who all the dim way doth illume,
And bids me look beyond the tomb
    The larger life to live?—
Not what I do believe,
But Whom!
Not what, but Whom!

—John Oxenham

(Used by permission of the Author)

Incarnate Love

O Love of God incarnate,
    Who comest from above,
To show us God the Father
    In human life of love,
God's love to earth thou bringest
    That men may see in thee
How like man is the Father,
    How like God man may be.

O Love of God incarnate,
    Life bearer sent to men,
Who drinks at thy deep fountain
    Shall never thirst again:
God's life to earth thou bringest,
    And, though the thorn-path trod
Led thee to death on Calvary,
    Thou wast the Son of God!

O Love of God incarnate,
    Thy resurrection hour
Revealed the life eternal,
    And robbed death of its power:
Enthroned on high thou reignest
    That men may share with thee
Thy life, thy love, thy glory,
    And live eternally.

O Love of God incarnate,
  Thou ever-living Word,
Through whom the Father speaketh,
  In whom man's voice is heard,
In thee all love and wisdom,
  Divine and human, meet;
When God through thee hath spoken,
  Love's message is complete!

—*Wilbur Fisk Tillett*

(Used by permission)

Not I

Not I, but Christ
Be honored, loved, exalted;
  Not I, but Christ
Be seen, be known, be heard;
  Not I, but Christ
In every look and action;
  Not I, but Christ
In every thought and word.

—*Anonymous*

None of Self and All of Thee

Oh, the bitter shame and sorrow
  That a time could ever be
When I let the Saviour's pity
Plead in vain, and proudly answered,
  "All of self and none of Thee."

Yet He found me; I beheld Him
  Bleeding on the accursed tree;
Heard Him pray, "Forgive them, Father;"
And my wistful heart said faintly,
  "Some of self and some of Thee."

Day by day, His tender mercy,
  Healing, helping, full and free,
Sweet and strong, and, oh, so patient,
Brought me lower, while I whispered,
  "Less of self and more of Thee."

Higher than the highest heavens,
  Deeper than the deepest sea,
Lord, *Thy love* at last has conquered;
Grant me now my soul's desire,
  "None of self and all of Thee."
                            —*Theodore Monod*

Our Master

We may not climb the heavenly steeps
  To bring the Lord Christ down;
In vain we search the lowest deeps,
  For Him no depths can drown.

But warm, sweet, tender, even yet
  A present help is He;
And faith has still its Olivet,
  And love its Galilee.

Through Him the first fond prayers are said
  Our lips of childhood frame;
The last low whispers of our dead
  Are burdened with His name.

O Lord and Master of us all,
  Whate'er our name or sign,
We own Thy sway, we hear Thy call,
  We test our lives by Thine!
                            —*John G. Whittier*

The Way; The Truth; The Life

Without the Way, there can be no going;
Without the Truth, there can be no knowing;
Without the Life, there can be no growing.

Since Christ is the Way, we ought to walk in him;
Since Christ is the Truth, we ought to trust in him;
Since Christ is the Life, we ought to live in him.

Thou who art the Way, lead us;
Thou who art the Truth, teach us;
Thou who art the Life, continue to live in us and love us.
—*Samuel Judson Porter*

The True Apostolate

The glory of Love is brightest when the glory of self is dim,
And they have the most compelled me who most have
        pointed to Him.
They have held me, stirred me, swayed me,—I have hung
        on their every word
Till I fain would arise and follow, not them, not them,—
        but their Lord!
—*Ruby T. Weyburn*

The Greatest Person In the Universe

"That I May Know Him"

Christ is the Fact of facts, the Bible's Theme,
Who stands alone, august, unique, supreme;
The Bread of Life, who meets the need of men,
Who comes to all, o'er field, and moor, and fen;
The Man of Pain, who feels all human pain,
And slakes the thirst, and turns all loss to gain,
He is the God, all light from Him doth gleam,
He is the Man of men, beyond all dream;
He is the God of Love, all love Divine,
He is the Hand of Power, all strength sublime;
From Him all things come forth, in Him consist,
To Him all tend, and all by Him subsist.
The Book, it speaks of Him, the Christ reveals,
The eyes that close to Him, all truth conceal;
He is the Gospel's Theme—He died for all,
His death alone can free from sin's enthrall;

His resurrection life, the might of might,
His reign within the soul, the life of right;
His peace within the heart, the calm of love,
His joy untold, the thrill from realms above;
His love, the fire that burns within the Fane,
His promises, the world's refreshing rain;
The Spirit came, the outcome of His death,
The power of God, His grace and living breath;
He's All! the Visibility of God,
And so I sing of Him and onward plod.

—Daniel L. Marsh, D. D.

Unchanging Jesus

All is dying; hearts are breaking
    Which to ours were once fast bound;
And the lips have ceased from speaking,
    Which once uttered such sweet sound;
And the arms are powerless lying,
    Which were our support and stay;
And the eyes are dim and dying,
    Which once watched us night and day.

Everything we love and cherish
    Hastens onward to the grave;
Earthly joys and pleasures perish,
    And whate'er the world e'er gave:
All is fading, all is fleeing,
    Earthly flames must cease to glow.
Earthly beings cease from being,
    Earthly blossoms cease to blow.

Yet unchanged, while all decayeth,
    Jesus stands upon the dust;
"Lean on Me alone," He sayeth,
    "Hope and love and firmly trust!"
Oh, abide, abide with Jesus,
    Who Himself forever lives,
Who from death eternal frees us,
    Yea, Who life eternal gives!

—Spitta, tr. by R. Massie

The Blessed Name

There is no name so sweet on earth,
  No name so sweet in heaven,
The name before His wondrous birth
  To Christ the Saviour given.

O Jesus, by Thy matchless name,
  Thy grace shall fail us never;
To-day as yesterday the same,
  We'll bless Thy name forever.

For there's no name ear ever heard
  So dear, so sweet as Jesus.
We love to sing of Christ our King
  And hail Him, blessed Jesus.
                    —*George W. Bethune*

What Christ Is To Us

The Shield from every dart;
The Balm for every smart;
The Sharer of each load;
Companion on the road.

The Door into the fold;
The Anchor that will hold;
The Shepherd of the sheep;
The Guardian of my sleep.

The Friend with Whom I talk;
The Way by which I walk;
The Light to show the way;
The Strength for every day.

The Source of my delight;
The Song to cheer the night;
The Thought that fills my mind;
The Best of All to find—is Jesus!
                    —*Anonymous*

CHRISTMAS

The Nativity

Hark, the herald angels sing,
"Glory to the new-born King,
Peace on earth, and mercy mild;
God and sinners reconciled."

Joyful, all ye nations, rise;
Join the triumphs of the skies;
With the angelic host proclaim,
"Christ is born in Bethlehem."

See, He lay His glory by;
Born that man no more may die;
Born to raise the sons of earth;
Born to give them second birth.

Hail, the heaven-born Prince of Peace!
Hail, the Son of Righteousness,
Light and life to all He brings,
Ris'n with healing in His wings.

Let us then with angels sing,
"Glory to the new-born King!
Peace on earth, and mercy mild;
God and sinners reconciled."

—Charles Wesley

Christmas Bells

I heard the bells, on Christmas Day,
Their old, familiar carols play,
    And wild and sweet
    The words repeat
Of peace on earth, good will to men.

And thought how, as the day had come,
The belfries of all Christendom
    Had rolled along
    The unbroken song
Of peace on earth, good will to men.

Till ringing, singing on its way,
The world revolved from day to day,
    A voice, a chime,
    A chant sublime
Of peace on earth, good will to men.

Then pealed the bells more loud and deep:
"God is not dead; nor doth He sleep;
    The wrong shall fail,
    The right prevail,
With peace on earth, good will to men."

—Longfellow

Christmas Everywhere

Everywhere, everywhere, Christmas tonight!
Christmas in lands of the fir-tree and pine,
Christmas in lands of the palm-tree and vine,
Christmas where snow peaks stand solemn and white,
Christmas where cornfields stand sunny and bright.
Christmas where children are hopeful and gay,
Christmas where old men are patient and gray,
Christmas where peace, like a dove in his flight,
Broods o'er brave men in the thick of the fight;
Everywhere, everywhere, Christmas tonight!
For the Christ-child who comes is the Master of all;
No palace too great, no cottage too small.

—Phillips Brooks

(From "Christmas Songs and Easter Carols." Copyright, 1903, by
E. P. Dutton & Co.)

O Little Town of Bethlehem

O little town of Bethlehem,
  How still we see thee lie!
Above thy deep and dreamless sleep
  The silent stars go by.
Yet in thy dark streets shineth
  The everlasting Light:
The hopes and fears of all the years
  Are met in thee tonight.

For Christ is born of Mary,
  And gathered all above,
While mortals sleep, the angels keep
  Their watch of wondering love.
O morning stars, together
  Proclaim the holy birth,
And praises sing to God the King.
  And peace to men on earth.

O holy Child of Bethlehem!
  Descend to us, we pray;
Cast out our sin, and enter in.
  Be born in us today.
We hear the Christmas angels
  The great glad tidings tell;
O come to us, abide with us,
  Our Lord Immanuel!

—Phillips Brooks

(From "Christmas Songs and Easter Carols." Copyright, 1903, by
E. P. Dutton & Co.)

A Happy Christmas

A happy Christmas to you!
  For the Prince of peace is come,
And His reign is full of blessings,
  Their very crown and sum;

No earthly calm can ever last,
'Tis but the lull before the blast;
    But His great peace
    Shall still increase
In mighty all-rejoicing sway;
His kingdom in thy heart shall never pass away.

—*Frances Ridley Havergal*

Christmas Carol

From the starry heav'ns descending
    Herald angels in their flight,
        Nearer winging,
        Clearer singing,
    Thrilled with harmony the night:
"Glory, glory in the highest!"
    Sounded yet and yet again,
        Sweeter, clearer,
        Fuller, nearer—
"Peace on earth, good will to men!"

Shepherds in the field abiding,
    Roused from sleep, that gladsome morn,
        Saw the glory
        Heard the story
    That the Prince of Peace was born:
"Glory, glory in the highest!"
    Sang the angel choir again,
        Nearer winging,
        Clearer singing:
"Peace on earth, good will to men!"

Swept the angel singers onward,
    Died the song upon the air;
        But the glory
        Of that story
Grows and triumphs everywhere;

And when glow the Yuletide heavens,
  Seems that glorious song again
    Floating nearer,
    Sweeter, clearer—
"Peace on earth, good will to men!"

—*J. R. Newell*

A Thousand Years Have Come

A thousand years have come and gone,
  And near a thousand more,
Since happier light from heaven shone
  Than ever shone before,
And in the hearts of old and young
  A joy most joyful stirred,
That sent such news from tongue to tongue
  As ears had never heard.

And we are glad, and we will sing,
  As in the days of yore;
Come all, and hearts made ready bring,
  To welcome back once more
The day when first on wintry earth
  A summer change began,
And, dawning in a lowly birth,
  Uprose the Light of man.

—*Thomas T. Lynch*

The Heavenly Stranger

No warm, downy pillow His sweet head pressed;
No soft silken garments His fair form dressed;
  He lay in a manger,
  This heavenly Stranger,
The precious Lord Jesus, the wonderful child.

No jubilant clang of rejoicing bell
The glorious news to the world did tell;
  But angels from glory
  Sang sweetly the story
Of Bethlehem's Stranger, the Saviour of men.

Thou heavenly Stranger, so gentle and mild,
Though born in a manger, the Father's own Child,
We'll worship before Thee
And praise and adore Thee,
And sing the glad story again and again.

—Ada Blenkhorn

CHURCH

At Church Next Sunday

If I knew you and you knew me,
How little trouble there would be.
We pass each other on the street,
But just come out and let us meet,
        At church next Sunday.

Each one intends to do what's fair,
And treat his neighbor on the square,
But he may not quite understand
Why you don't take him by the hand
        At church next Sunday.

This world is sure a busy place,
And we must hustle in the race.
For social hours some are not free
The six week days, but all should be
        At church next Sunday.

We have an interest in our town,
The dear old place must not go down;
We want to push good things along.
And we can help some if we're strong
        At church next Sunday.

Don't knock and kick and slam and slap
At everybody on the map,
But push and pull and boost and boom
And use up all the standing room
        At church next Sunday.

—Anonymous

A Little Rhyme and a Little Reason

If a man would be a soldier, he'd expect, of course, to fight;
And he couldn't be an author if he didn't try to write.
So it isn't common logic, doesn't have a real, true ring,
That a man to be a Christian doesn't have to do a thing.

If a man would be a hunter, he must go among the trees;
And he couldn't be a sailor if he wouldn't sail the seas.
How strange for any member of a church to think that he
Can stay away from worship and a worthy member be!

When you join associations, you must pay up all your dues;
And you pay for all you purchase, from your hat down to
    your shoes.
There are social clubs for women, and the same for men and
    boys,
But the members all expect to pay for what each one enjoys.

Then how is it that the members of a church can sit in pews,
And expect some few to run it without others paying dues?
The costs of operation must be met in church the same
As in home or corporation or in work of any name.

Let us honestly consider why this difference we find,
Between our church relations and every other kind.
Our business obligations MUST be met, the laws provide;
But the church is not insistent, so we let the matter slide.

May we undertake our duties for our church and for our
    Lord
With such measure of devotion as accords with His own
    Word.
If our human obligations thus are recognized, why then
Surely God should have our service now and evermore.
    Amen.

—*Rev. Henry Anstadt, D. D.*

(Copyright, 1927, by The Duplex Envelope Company, Richmond,
Virginia. Used by permission)

Dedication

Thou, whose unmeasured temple stands,
  Built over earth and sea,
Accept the walls that human hands
  Have raised, O God, to Thee!

Lord, from Thine inmost glory send,
  Within these courts to bide,
The peace that dwelleth without end
  Serenely by Thy side!

May erring minds that worship here
  Be taught the better way;
And they who mourn, and they who fear,
  Be strengthened as they pray.

May faith grow firm, and love grow warm,
  And pure devotion rise,
While round these hallowed walls the storm
  Of earthborn passion dies.

—William Cullen Bryant
(By permission of D. Appleton & Co.)

Hymn of Dedication

Father, here a temple in Thy name we build;
Ever may Thy purpose in it be fulfilled.
Circled by Thy kindness, and Thy smile above,
May it stand for worship, service, faith and love.

REFRAIN

Father, here a temple in Thy name we build:
Ever may Thy purpose in it be fulfilled.

Here may all who enter, feel Thy presence near,
Here the Holy Spirit bring a message clear.
Of Thy Son, beloved, child and youth be taught;
Measured by His standard, character be wrought.

May the sad find comfort, weary ones find rest,
Here the sick and lonely be with friendship blest;
Strength for those who falter, faith for all who doubt,
May Thy love, O Father, bind this place about.

—Elizabeth E. Scantlebury

Just Like Me

What sort of a church would our church be
If every member were just like me?
Better or worse would our church be
If every member were just like me?
Were every member of our church to be
Just such a member as Christ would see,
What changes would come to you and to me,
And the gain to our church—what would it be?

—P. W. Sinks

An Angel Unawares

If after kirk ye bide a wee,
    There's some would like to speak to ye.
If after kirk ye rise and flee,
    We'll all seem cold and stiff to ye.
That one that's in the seat wi' ye,
    Is stranger here than you, may be;
Add you your soul unto our prayers;
    Be you our angel unawares.

—Anonymous

CONSECRATION

Take My Life and Let It Be

Take my life and let it be
Consecrated, Lord, to thee;
Take my moments and my days,
Let them flow in endless praise;

Take my hands and let them move
At the impulse of thy love;
Take my feet and let them be
Swift and beautiful for thee.

Take my voice and let me sing,
Always, only, for my King.
Take my lips and let them be
Filled with messages from thee.
Take my silver and my gold;
Not a mite would I withhold.
Take my intellect and use
Every power as thou shalt choose.

Take my will and make it thine;
It shall be no longer mine.
Take my heart, it is thine own;
It shall be thy royal throne.
Take my love, my Lord, I pour
At thy feet its treasure-store.
Take myself, and I will be
Ever, only, all for thee.

—*Frances Ridley Havergal*

What Shall We Render

God wants our best. He in the far-off ages
Once claimed the firstling of the flock, the finest of the
    wheat;
And still He asks His own, with gentlest pleading,
To lay their highest hopes and brighest talents at His feet.
He'll not forget the feeblest service, humblest love;
He only asks that of our store, we give the best we have.

Christ gives the best. He takes the hearts we offer
And fills them with His glorious beauty, joy and peace,
And in His Service as we're growing stronger
The calls to grand achievements e'er increase.
The richest gifts for us, on earth or in heaven above,
Are hid in Christ. In Jesus we receive the best we have.

—*Anonymous*

The Yielded Life

What is a Yielded Life?
  'Tis one at God's command,
For Him to mold, to form, to use
Or do with it as He may choose,
  Resistless in His hand.

What is a Yielded Life?
  A life whose only will,
When into blest subjection brought—
In every deed and aim and thought,
  Seeks just to do His Will.

What is a Yielded Life?
  A life which love has won,
And in surrender full, complete,
Lays all with gladness at the feet
  Of God's most Holy Son.

—W. A. G.

O Lord, I Come Pleading

O Lord, I come pleading and praying to Thee,
I'm seeking salvation so full and so free,
I'm hungering and thirsting Thy fulness to know,
That I may be washed and made whiter than snow.

I fully surrender my will and my all,
Myself and possessions are Thine at Thy call,
I'll follow wherever Thy Spirit doth show,
If Thou wilt the fulness of blessing bestow.

O come, blessed Spirit, and dwell Thou within,
And sanctify, purge me, and cleanse me from sin,
Endue me for service with power from on high,
O God, to the world and the flesh let me die.

Oh, now I'm believing and trusting in Thee;
My offering's accepted—by faith I can see;
I'm resting just now in Thine infinite love,
Thy Spirit comes in like a heavenly dove.

—James Gilchrist Lawson

Nearer, My God, To Thee

Nearer, my God, to Thee,
  Nearer to Thee!
E'en though it be a cross
  That raiseth me;
Still all my song shall be,
Nearer, my God, to Thee,
  Nearer to Thee!

Though like the wanderer,
  The sun gone down,
Darkness be over me,
  My rest a stone;
Yet in my dreams I'd be
Nearer, my God, to Thee,
  Nearer to Thee!

There let the way appear
  Steps unto Heaven,
All that Thou sendest me
  In mercy given;
Angels to beckon me
Nearer, my God, to Thee,
  Nearer to Thee!

Then with my waking thoughts
  Bright with Thy praise,
Out of my stony griefs,
  Bethel I'll raise;
So by my woes to be
Nearer, my God, to Thee,
  Nearer to Thee!

Or if, on joyful wing,
  Cleaving the sky,
Sun, moon and stars forgot,
  Upward I fly,
Still all my song shall be,
Nearer, my God, to Thee,
  Nearer to Thee!

—Sarah Flower Adams

CONTRITION

Recessional

God of our fathers, known of old,
  Lord of our far-flung battle line,
Beneath whose awful hand we hold
  Dominion over palm and pine,
Lord God of Hosts, be with us yet,
Lest we forget, lest we forget!

The tumult and the shouting dies,
  The captains and the kings depart;
Still stands thy ancient sacrifice,
  A humble and a contrite heart.
Lord God of Hosts, be with us yet,
Lest we forget, lest we forget!

Far called, our navies melt away,
  On dune and headland sinks the fire;
Lo, all our pomp of yesterday
  Is one with Nineveh and Tyre!
Judge of the Nations, spare us yet,
Lest we forget, lest we forget!

If, drunk with sight of power, we loose
  Wild tongues that have not Thee in awe,
Such boastings as the Gentiles use—
  Or lesser breeds without the law—
Lord God of Hosts, be with us yet,
Lest we forget, lest we forget!

For heathen heart that puts her trust
  In reeking tube and iron shard,
All valiant dust that builds on dust,
  And guarding, calls not Thee to guard,
For frantic boast and foolish word,
Thy mercy on Thy people, Lord!   Amen.
                                    —*Rudyard Kipling*

Oh, If They Only Knew!

Some people think I think I'm good.
Oh, if they only understood!
Could they but draw aside the screen
Of shielding clay that stands between,
And see the penitent within
That craves so oft release from sin;

If some kind angel could reveal
The sense of guilt and shame I feel
Because my heart will ope to things
Whose very entrance blights and stings;
Oh, if they only, only knew
The grace it takes to just ring true!

If they could understand my need,
And hear what I confess and plead,
And know how fully I depend
Upon my precious Lord and Friend;
I wonder, would they call such dress
The mantle of self-righteousness?

—*Edith L. Mapes*

CO-WORKERS WITH GOD

Your Place

Is your place a small place?
   Tend it with care!—
      He set you there.

Is your place a large place?
   Guard it with care!—
      He set you there.

Whate'er your place, it is
   Not yours alone, but His
      That set you there.

—*John Oxenham*

(By permission of the Author)

"Laborers Together With God"

Helpless am I indeed
    To right earth's grievous wrong,
To help earth's bitter need;
    But thou, my God, art strong.

Too weak I am, I know,
    To fight the foes within;
But thou dost strength bestow
    That I may conquer sin.

Naught for life's work have I
    But feeble human sense;
Thou dost my need supply
    From thy omnipotence.

Oh, partnership divine,
    That thou dost work with me!
What wealth and power are mine,
    Since I may work with thee!

—*Lucy Alice Perkins*

DEATH

If To Die—

If to die is to rise in power from the husk of the earth-sown
    wheat,
If to die is to rise in glory from the dust of the incomplete,
If death fills the hand with fresh cunning and fits it with
    perfect tool,
And grants to the mind full power for the tasks of its great-
    est school,
If death gives new breath to the runner and wings to the
    imprisoned soul
To mount with a song of the morning towards the limitless
    reach of its goal,

If to die is to throb with the surges of life that eternal
   abides,
And to thrill with the inflowing currents of infinite love's
   great tides,
If to die is to see with clear vision all mysteries revealed,
All beauty to sense unfolded, and the essence of joy un-
   sealed,
If death is the end to all sorrow and crying and anxious
   care,
If death gives fulness for longing, and the answer to every
   prayer,
If to die is to greet all the martyrs and prophets and sages
   of old,
And to walk again by still waters with the flock of our own
   little fold,
If to die is to join in hosannas to a risen and reigning Lord,
And to feast with him at his table on the bread and wine of
   his board,
If to die is to enter a city and be hailed as a child of its
   king,—
O grave, where soundeth thy triumph?   O death, where
   hideth thy sting?

—Myrtle Romilu

Emancipation

*"We know that if the earthly house of our tabernacle be dissolved,
we have a building from God, a house not made with hands, eternal,
in the heavens."—II Cor. 5:1.*

Why be afraid of death as though your life were breath?
Death but anoints your eyes with clay.   O glad surprise!

Why should you be forlorn?   Death only husks the corn.
Why should you fear to meet the thresher of the wheat?

Is sleep a thing to dread?   Yet sleeping you are dead
Till you awake and rise, here, or beyond the skies.

Why should it be a wrench to leave your wooden bench?
Why not, with happy shout, run home when school is out?

The dear ones left behind!   O, foolish one and blind;
A day—and you will meet: a night—and you will greet!

This is the death of Death, to breathe away a breath
And know the end of strife and taste the deathless life,

And joy without a fear, and smile without a tear,
And work, nor care to rest, and find the last the best.

—*Maltbie D. Babcock*

The Kiss of God

It was not death to me,
Nor aught the least like falling into sleep.
It was nothing to joy upon
Nor yet to weep.
It was an infinitely perfect peace
Wherein the world entrancéd
Stood quite still
Outside of time and space:
And like a changeless, everchanging face
Looked kindly on me
As I lay
And waited on His will.
It was not night
Nor day—
But bright with rainbow colors
Of an everlasting dawn
Down from the golden glory light
That shone in His great eyes.
The mysteries of earth
Lay open like a book,
And I could read
But slowly, as a small child reads
With an often upward look
That pleads
For help—still doubtful of the truth
Until he sees it mirrored
In the answering eyes of Love.

So I looked up to God
And while I held my breath,
I saw Him slowly nod,
And knew—as I had never known aught else,
With certainty sublime and passionate,
Shot through and through
With sheer unutterable bliss.
I knew
There was no death but this
God's kiss.
And then the waking to an everlasting Love.
　　　　　　　　　　　　—G. A. Studdert-Kennedy

The Great Victory

There is no death, O child divine,
　For One has cross'd the fearsome vale,
And with His radiance made it shine;
　You, too, can cross—you cannot fail.

There is no death; an angel hand,
　Soft-petaled, shuts our worldly eyes,
And opes them in a fairer land,
　A brighter world beyond the skies.

There is no death; why should we pine?
　The sun that sets shall rise once more,
And we shall live a life sublime,
　Resplendent, on that wondrous shore.
　　　　　　　　　　　　—R. V. Gilbert

"He Will Give Them Back"

We are quite sure
That he will give them back—bright, pure and beautiful—
We know he will but keep
Our own and his until we fall asleep.
We know he does not mean
To break the strands reaching between
The Here and There.

He does not mean—though heaven be fair—
To change the spirits entering there that they forget
The eyes upraised and wet,
The lips too still for prayer,
The mute despair.

He will not take
The spirits which he gave, and make
The glorified so new
That they are lost to me and you.

I do believe
They will receive
Us—you and me—and be so glad
To meet us, that when most I would grow sad
I just begin to think about that gladness,
And the day
When they shall tell us all about the way
That they have learned to go—
Heaven's pathway show.

My lost, my own, and I
Shall have so much to see together by and by.
I do believe that just the same sweet face,
But glorified, is waiting in the place
Where we shall meet, if only I
Am counted worthy in that by and by.
I do believe that God will give a sweet surprise
To tear-stained saddened eyes,
And that this his heaven will be
Most glad, most tided through with joy for you and me,
As we have suffered most.

God never made
Spirit for spirit, answering shade for shade,
And placed them side by side—
So wrought in one, though separate, mystified—
And meant to break
The quivering threads between. When we shall wake,
I am quite sure, we shall be very glad
That for a little while we were so sad.

                    —*Georgiana Holmes (George Klingle)*

Within the Veil

They never seem to be far away,
  The loved and dear who have left my side;
A breath, that the sunlight shall lift one day,
  Floateth between, their forms to hide.
I saw them last with their faces pale,
  As the angel arms were about them thrown;
I shall see them again, within the veil,
  In the glory that mortal hath never known.

When morn is fair in her silver mists,
  Or eve is dark with her shadows gray,
I think how royal with amethysts
  And pearl and gold is their shining day.
In the household work that they used to share,
  The thought of them is a bit of leaven,
And holier groweth each homely care
  That catcheth a gleam from the light of heaven.

They are only gone where our Jesus is,
  And never can that be far away;
They stand in his presence. Oh, perfect bliss,
  To dwell in the light of his face for aye!
Oft in prayer have we felt him near,
  Oft have we walked in his guiding hand;
They cannot lose him in doubt or fear,
  And therefore the joy of the better land.

Why should they seem to be far away,
  Loved and dear, for whom Jesus died?
White as a star is our hope one day
  To enter, and with them be satisfied.
Only a step to the clear noon-day,
  Out of our darkness, that is all!
Only a veil, that shall lift away,
  When, soft as zephyr, his touch shall fall.
                              —*Margaret E. Sangster*
          (Used by permission)

"Precious in the Sight of the Lord . . ."

Precious, Oh, how precious is that blessed sleep,
Folded in His bosom, wrapped in slumber deep;
None but Jesus giveth rest so true and sweet
For the weary body and the way-worn feet.

Precious, Oh, how precious, He alone can know
What a blessed respite after human woe;
Only He can measure their eternal gain,
When they leave for ever earthly care and pain.

Precious, Oh, how precious, armour here laid down,
Warfare here accomplished, won the victor's crown;
Gained His sweet approval and His welcome smile,
For the patient labour of this little while.

Precious, Oh, how precious, to behold His face,
Ever to be with Him and to praise His grace;
Ah, when Jesus giveth His beloved sleep,
'Tis the tenderest token of His love so deep.

—Anonymous

Not Lost, But Gone Before

How mournful seems, in broken dreams,
    The memory of the day,
When icy Death hath sealed the breath
    Of some dear form of clay.

When pale, unmoved, the face we loved,
    The face we thought so fair,
And the hand lies cold, whose fervent hold
    Once charmed away despair.

Oh, what could heal the grief we feel
    For hopes that come no more,
Had we ne'er heard the Scripture word,
    "Not lost, but gone before."

Oh sadly yet with vain regret
 The widowed heart must yearn;
And mothers weep their babes asleep
 In the sunlight's vain return.

The brother's heart shall rue to part
 From the one through childhood known;
And the orphan's tears lament for years
 A friend and father gone.

For death and life, with ceaseless strife,
 Beat wild on this world's shore,
And all our calm is in that balm,
 "Not lost, but gone before."

Oh! world wherein nor death, nor sin,
 Nor weary warfare dwells;
Their blessed home we parted from
 With sobs and sad farewells.

Where eyes awake, for whose dear sake
 Our own with tears grow dim,
And faint accords of dying words
 Are changed for heaven's sweet hymn;

Oh! there at last, life's trials past,
 We'll meet our loved once more,
Whose feet have trod the path to God—
 "Not lost, but gone before."
                    —*Hon. Caroline Elizabeth Norton*

Crossing the Bar

Sunset and evening star,
 And one clear call for me,
And may there be no moaning of the bar,
 When I put out to sea.

But such a tide as moving seems asleep,
 Too full for sound and foam,
When that which drew from out the boundless deep
 Turns again home.

Twilight and evening bell,
    And after that the dark!
And may there be no sadness of farewell,
    When I embark;

For tho' from out our bourne of time and place
    The flood may bear me far,
I hope to see my Pilot face to face
    When I have crost the bar.

                    —*Alfred, Lord Tennyson*

A Dead Past (?)

Not so, for living yet are those
    Who long since passed away;
They live within our memories
    Yes, there they live alway.

Their look of love yet still remains,
    The words they spoke, we hear,
And in a corner of our heart
    Their face and form appear.

Not only those we know and love
    But others passed along,
Who yet are living by their deeds,
    And lead a mighty throng.

A Dead Past? No that cannot be,
    A past lives through the years,
Gives hope and comfort day by day
    By faith, gives hopes to fears.

The Mighty Prince of Peace yet lives
    We feel Him close at hand,
His Word controls the universe
    It yields to His command.

I cannot think of a Dead Past,
    It often speaks to me
And in my soul I hear its words,
    Hence alive the Past must be.

                    —*C. C. Munson*

The Burial of Moses

By Nebo's lonely mountain,
  On this side Jordan's wave,
In a vale of the land of Moab,
  There lies a lonely grave.
But no man dug that sepulchre,
  And no man saw it e'er;
For the angels of God upturned the sod,
  And laid the dead man there.

That was the grandest funeral
  That ever passed on earth;
But no man heard the trampling,
  Or saw the train go forth.
Noiselessly as the daylight
  Comes, when the night is done,
Or the crimson streak on ocean's cheek
  Fades in the setting sun;

Noiselessly as the spring-time
  Her crest of verdure waves,
And all the trees on all the hills
  Open their thousand leaves;
So without sound of music,
  Or voice of them that wept,
Silently down from the mountain's crown
  That grand procession swept.

Perchance some bald old eagle
  On gray Beth-peor's height,
Out of his rocky eyrie,
  Looked on the wondrous sight;
Perchance some lion, stalking,
  Still shuns the hallowed spot;
For beast and bird have seen and heard
  That which man knoweth not.

But when the warrior dieth,
  His comrades in the war,
With arms reversed and muffled drums
  Follow the funeral car;

They show the banners taken,
  They tell his battles won,
And after him lead his matchless steed,
  While peals the minute gun.

And the noblest of the land
  They lay the sage to rest;
And give the bard an honored place,
  With costly marble drest,
In the great minister's transept height,
  Where lights like glory fall,
While the sweet choir sings, and the organ rings
  Along the emblazoned wall.

This was the bravest warrior
  That ever buckled sword;
This the most gifted poet
  That ever breathed a word;
And never earth's philosopher
  Traced with his golden pen,
On the deathless page, words half so sage,
  As he wrote down for men.

And had he not high honor?
  The hill-side for his pall,
To lie in state while angels wait,
  With stars for tapers tall;
The dark rock-pines like tossing plumes
  Over his bier to wave,
And God's own hand in that lonely land
  To lay him in the grave:

In that deep grave without a name,
  Whence his uncoffined clay
Shall break again—most wondrous thought!
  Before the judgement day;
And stand, with glory wrapt around,
  On the hills he never trod,
And speak of the strife that won our life
  Through Christ the Incarnate God.

O lonely tomb in Moab's land!
O dark Beth-peor's hill!
Speak to these curious hearts of ours,
    And teach them to be still:
God hath his mysteries of grace,
    Ways that we cannot tell,
He hides them deep, like the secret sleep
    Of him he loved so well.

—Cecil Frances Alexander

Away

I can not say, and I will not say,
That he is dead—he is just away.
With a cheery smile and a wave of the hand,
He has wandered into an unknown land,
And left us dreaming, how very fair
It needs must be, since he lingers there.
And you—O you, who so wildly yearn
For the old-time step and the glad return,
Think of him faring on, as dear
In the love of There as the love of Here.
Think of him as the same, I say;
He is not dead—he is just away.

—James Whitcomb Riley

(From "Afterwhiles." Copyright, 1887 and 1915. Used by permission
of The Bobbs-Merrill Company)

Just Passing

Passing out of the shadow
    Into a purer light;
Stepping behind the curtain,
    Getting a clearer sight; . .

Passing out of the shadow
    Into eternal day.
Why do we call it dying,
    This sweet going away?

—Anonymous

The Satisfying Portion

'Tis religion that can give
Sweetest comfort while we live,
'Tis religion must supply
Solid comfort when we die.

After death, its joys will be
Lasting as eternity;
Be the living God my Friend,
Then my joys shall never end.

—Anonymous

EASTER

On Easter Morning

What tidings of reverent gladness are voiced by the bells
    that ring
A summons to men to gather to-day in the courts of the
    King!
"He is risen!" O glorious message! "He lives, who once
    was dead!"
And hearts that were heavy with sorrow hear and are com-
    forted.

We come to our dear Lord's altar. What brightness greets
    us there!
The gloom of the winter has vanished, and beauty is every-
    where.
From the censer-cups of the lilies rise scents of myrrh and
    balm,
And the soul, like a lark, soars upward winged with the
    Easter psalm.

O beautiful, beautiful lilies, what truths you typify:
You seemed to die in the autumn, and yet you did not die.
And on this Easter morning while joyful voices sing
You repeat to all the lesson of the miracle of spring.

"Alleluia," the choir is chanting with joyous, jubilant voice.
"The Lord is risen, is risen! Rejoice, rejoice, rejoice!"
From the tomb in which men laid Him the stone is rolled
    away,
And lo! the Christ they sing of is here in our midst to-day.
                    —*Eben E. Rexford*

An Easter Song

A song of sunshine through the rain,
Of Spring across the snow;
A balm to heal the hurts of pain,
A peace surpassing woe.
Lift up your heads, ye sorrowing ones,
And be ye glad at heart,
For Calvary and Easter Day,
Earth's saddest day and gladdest day,
Were just three days apart!

With shudder of despair and loss
The world's deep heart was wrung,
As, lifted high upon His cross,
The Lord of Glory hung—
When rocks were rent, and ghostly forms
Stole forth in street and mart;
But Calvary and Easter Day,
Earth's blackest day and whitest day,
Were just three days apart.
                    —*Susan Coolidge*

If Easter Be Not True

"If Christ hath not been raised your faith is vain."—Paul.

If Easter be not true,
Then all the lilies low must lie;
The Flanders poppies fade and die;
The spring must lose her fairest bloom
For Christ were still within the tomb—
If Easter be not true.

If Easter be not true,
Then faith must mount on broken wing;
Then hope no more immortal spring;
Then hope must lose her mighty urge;
Life prove a phantom, death a dirge—
    If Easter be not true.

If Easter be not true,
'Twere foolishness the cross to bear;
He died in vain who suffered there;
What matter though we laugh or cry,
Be good or evil, live or die,
    If Easter be not true?

If Easter be not true—
But it is true, and Christ is risen!
And mortal spirit from its prison
Of sin and death with him may rise!
Worthwhile the struggle, sure the prize,
    Since Easter, aye, is true!
                    —*Henry H. Barstow, D.D.*

Christ Is Risen!

Come, rejoice, 'tis Easter Day!
Lo, the stone is rolled away!
    Empty lies His tomb.

Death hath lost its bitter sting—
Ring, ye bells of Easter, ring!
    Christ is risen today.

Lo, He comes to you and me,
Bringing immortality,
    That we, too, may live.

Priceless gift from Christ our King!
Ring, ye bells of Easter, ring!
    Christ is risen today.
                    —*Mrs. D. H. Dugan*

A Song at Easter

If this bright lily
   Can live once more,
And its white promise
   Be as before,
Why can not the great stone
   Be moved from His door?

If the green grass
   Ascend and shake
Year after year,
   And blossoms break
Again and again
   For April's sake,

Why can not He,
   From the dark and mold,
Show us again
   His manifold
And gleaming glory,
   A stream of gold?

Faint heart, be sure
   These things must be.
See the new bud
   On the old tree! . . .
If flowers can wake,
   Oh, why not He?

          —*Charles Hanson Towne*

Easter Beatitudes

Blessed are they of the Easter faith,
For theirs is the risen Lord;
For them He lives, and to them He gives
The fountain of life restored.

Blessed are they of the Easter cheer,
For theirs is the burning heart;
For them the tomb is bereft of gloom,
They walk with their Lord apart.

Blessed are they of the Easter hope,
For theirs is the open gate;
It swings through the tomb to that other room
Where the Lord and our loved ones wait.
                              —*Clarence M. Burkholder*

Because He Lives

Because He lives, I, too, shall live;
    The same life quickens me
That held His Spirit all secure
    Above the death-bound Tree.

Because He lives, I cannot die.
    Death signifies no loss;
My soul shall know but spirit-change
    Because He knew the Cross.

Because He lives, His Cross transmutes
    Death into Life, for me;
And failure, fear, disease, and death,
    Love crowns with victory.
                              —*Adele Lathrop*

Not In Vain

Hope we not in this life only.
    Christ Himself has made it plain
None who sleep in Him shall perish,
    And our faith is not in vain.
Not in vain our glad hosannas;
    Since we follow where He led,
Not in vain our Easter anthem:
    "Christ has risen from the dead!"
                              —*Anonymous*

Triumph

Up and down, o'er hill and valley,
  Sounds the Easter jubilee;
Breezes sing it—echoes fling it;
  Bursting bud, and leaf, and tree,—
Whispers of the life to be.

All the world is full of glory,
  All the bonds of death are riven,
Listen to the swelling chorus—
  Christ, the Lord, has risen! risen!
Sing, oh, earth,—fling wide the story,
  While the echoes ring, and ring,—
Pulsing—throbbing with the glory—
  Grave is conquered! Christ is King!

—*L. D. Stearns*

FAITH

The Light of Faith

No cloud can hide the glow of living faith,
Faith is a light which shines through night and day;
Its piercing beams are falling everywhere
To drive man's woes and fears away.

No thought can smite the beam of glowing faith,
Faith is a power which man can never hide;
Its currents every believing child can feel—
A living touch which makes one satisfied.

No world can wreck the way of Christian faith,
Faith is secure so long as man hath need;
It grows as leaven in the hearts of men
And thrives with every Christian deed.

No power can take the place of living faith;
Faith hath its laws, its living evidence;
It glows in hearts of cheer and hope,
Revealing with it God's great providence.

—General Edgar Dupree

If We Believed In God

If we believed in God, there would be light
Upon our pathway in the darkest night.

If we believed in God, there would be power
To foil the tempter in the sorest hour.

If we believed in God, there would be peace
In this world's warfare, ever to increase.

If we believed in God, there would be joy
Even in tears, that nothing could destroy.

If we believed in God, there would be love
To heal all wounds and lift the world above.

Lord Christ, be near us, that, beholding Thee,
We may believe in God and be set free!

—Jessie Wiseman Gibbs

Jesus Himself

I do not ask Thee, Lord, for outward sign,
  For portents in the earth or flaming sky;
It is enough to know that Thou art mine,
  And not far off, but intimately nigh.

No burning bush I need to speak Thy name,
  Or call me forward to the newer task;
Give me a burning heart, with love aflame,
  Which sees Thee everywhere, is all I ask.

No pillar-cloud I seek to mark my way
  Through all the windings of the trackless years;
Thou art my Guide, by night as well as day,
  To choose my path, and hush my foolish fears.

I do not look for fiery cloven tongues,
  To tell for me the pentecostal hour;
The Father's promise for all time belongs
  To him who seeks the Spirit's quickening power.

I do not ask for voices from the sky;
  The thunder-peal I might not understand;
But let me hear Thy whisper, It is I!
  Fear not the darkness, child, but take My hand!

What can I ask but Thine own Self, dear Lord?
  Omniscience and omnipotence are Thine.
Let but my will with Thy sweet will accord,
  And all Thou hast, and all Thou art is mine!
                                    —*Dr. Henry Burton*

A Prayer for Faith

I would not ask Thee that my days
  Should flow quite smoothly on and on;
Lest I should learn to love the world
  Too well, ere all my time was done.

I would not ask Thee that my work
  Should never bring me pain nor fear;
Lest I should learn to work alone,
  And never wish Thy presence near.

I would not ask Thee that my friends
  Should now and always constant be;
Lest I should learn to lay my faith
  In them alone, and not in Thee.

But I would ask Thee still to give
  By night my sleep, by day my bread,
And that the counsel of Thy Word
  Should shine and show the path to tread.

And I would ask a humble heart,
A changeless will to work and wake,
A firm faith in Thy providence,
The rest—'tis Thine to give or take.
—*Alfred Norris*

Why Doubt God's Word?

It is strange we trust each other,
And only doubt our Lord.
We take the word of mortals,
And yet distrust His word;
But oh, what light and glory
Would shine o'er all our days,
If we always would remember
God means just what He says.
—*Rev. A. B. Simpson*

I Will Believe

I will believe.
Though young hopes one by one have fled,
Though joy and love be all but dead,
Through all perplexity and dread,
I will believe.

I will believe,
Though memory be but a tomb,
Though light be lost in somber gloom,
The future ominous of doom,
I will believe.

I will believe,
That joy should greet each dawning day,
That error will not quench truth's ray,
That love is strength and triumph. Yea,
I will believe.

I will believe—
In honor, justice, truth, and right;
In laughter, gladness, song, and light.
In God's great beauty, I'll delight.
I will believe.

—*William H. Roberts*

All Needs Met

Grace that never can be told
    Flows for Jesus' sake;
No good thing does He withhold,
    Have we faith to take.
Rise, my soul, begin to live
Free to ask as He to give.
    Why so poor?
    A boundless store
Waits the asking;—want no more.

—*J. H. Sammis*

Faith

I will not doubt, though all my ships at sea
    Come drifting home with broken masts and sails;
    I shall believe the Hand which never fails,
From seeming evil worketh good to me;
    And, though I weep because those sails are battered,
    Still will I cry, while my best hopes lie shattered,
        "I trust in Thee."

I will not doubt, though all my prayers return
    Unanswered from the still, white realm above;
    I shall believe it is an all-wise Love
Which has refused those things for which I yearn;
    And though, at times, I can not keep from grieving,
    Yet the pure ardor of my fixed believing
        Undimmed shall burn.

I will not doubt, though sorrows fall like rain,
  And troubles swarm like bees about a hive;
  I shall believe the heights for which I strive
Are only reached by anguish and by pain;
  And, though I groan and tremble with my crosses,
  I yet shall see, through my severest losses,
      The greater gain.

I will not doubt; well anchored in the faith,
  Like some stanch ship, my soul braves every gale,
  So strong its courage that it will not fail
To breast the mighty, unknown sea of death.
  Oh, may I cry when body parts with spirit,
  "I do not doubt," so listening worlds may hear it
      With my last breath.
                              —*Ella Wheeler Wilcox*
(Used by permission of the W. B. Conkey Co., Hammond, Ind.)

I Believe

I believe.
That is to say,
The lenses of my soul sweep heaven alway.

I believe.
By this I mean
My mind is open to the things unseen.

I believe.
I firmly hold
To untimed truth, that never has been told.

I believe
What has been told
By men of worth, whom years do not make old.

I believe
Judea's Son,
Whose work continues, as it had begun.

I believe
To-morrow's Light
Is always burning 'round the rim of night.
— *J. B. Lawrence*

Satisfied

The shadow falls, the path I cannot trace;
　Fear not, my heart, if only faith abide;
If faith abide, thou conquerest time and place;
Some day, somewhere, thou shalt behold His face;
　O yearning heart, thou shalt be satisfied.

The shadow falls, the shadow cannot stay;
　Hope on, pray on, thou wilt not be denied:
Over the burnt-out embers of today
The golden morrow rises, and alway
　The promise stands—thou shalt be satisfied.

I cannot say to what far land I go,
　When I embark upon the foamless tide;
Or if I'll find the things I yearn for so,
Ever at all, O heart, I do not know:
　I only know thou shalt be satisfied.

I follow, moving toward the deep and vast,
　I follow hope, my star and faithful guide;
I shall rejoice in trails overpast,
And see that face, O heart of mine, at last,
　In whose dear look thou shalt be satisfied.
— *Sam V. Cole*

Unshrinking Faith

O for a faith that will not shrink,
　Though pressed by every foe;
That will not tremble on the brink
　Of any earthly woe.

That will not murmur or complain,
  Beneath the chastening rod,
But, in the hour of grief or pain,
  Will lean upon its God.

A faith that shines more bright and clear
  When tempests rage without;
And when in danger knows no fear,
  In darkness feels no doubt.

Lord, give us such a faith as this,
  And then, whate'er may come,
We'll taste e'en here the hallowed bliss
  Of an eternal home.

—*W. H. Balhurst*

FORGIVENESS

So Little and So Much

In that I have so greatly failed thee, Lord,
Have grace!
A place!
So little of fair work for thee have I
To show;
So much of what I might have done, I did not do.
Yet thou hast seen in me at times the will
For good,
Although so oft I did not do all that
I would.
Thou knowest me through and through, and yet thou canst,
Forgive.
Only in hope of thy redeeming grace
I live.

—*John Oxenham*

(Used by permission of the Author)

GIVING

How to Give

Give as you would if an angel
   Awaited your gift at the door.
Give as you would if tomorrow
   Found you where giving is o'er.

Give as you would to the Master
   If you met his loving look.
Give as you would of your substance
   If his hand the offering took.

—Anonymous

His Gift and Mine

Over against the treasury
He sits who gave Himself for me.
He sees the coppers that I give
Who gave His life that I might live.
He sees the silver I withhold
Who left for me His throne of gold,
Who found a manger for His bed,
Who had nowhere to lay His head;
He sees the gold I clasp so tight,
And I am debtor in His sight.

—Edith B. Gurley

How Long Shall I Give?

"Go break to the needy sweet charity's bread;
   For giving is living," the angel said.
"And must I be giving again and again?"
   My peevish and pitiless answer ran.
"Oh, no," said the angel, piercing me through,
"Just give till the Master stops giving to you."

—Anonymous

Love

Love gives its best
And knows the rest.
Its highest joy,
Is giving joy.
It knows no rest,
Until its best
Is given.
And that is why
Love at its best
Is Heaven.

—John Oxenham
(Used by permission of the Author)

Love's Prerogative

Love ever gives—
Forgives—outlives—
And ever stands
With open hands.
And while it lives,
It gives.
For this is Love's prerogative—
To give—and give—and give.

—John Oxenham
(Used by permission of the Author)

GOD

No Time For God

No time for God?
What fools we are, to clutter up
Our lives with common things
And leave without heart's gate
The Lord of life and Life itself—
Our God.

No time for God?
As soon to say, no time
To eat or sleep or love or die.
Take time for God
Or you shall dwarf your soul,
And when the angel death
Comes knocking at your door,
A poor mishapen thing you'll be
To step into eternity.

No time for God?
That day when sickness comes
Or trouble finds you out
And you cry out for God;
Will He have time for you?

No time for God?
Some day you'll lay aside
This mortal self and make your way
To worlds unknown,
And when you meet him face to face
Will He—Should He,
Have time for you?

—*Norman L. Trott*

God In the Nation's Life

Putting God in the Nation's life,
    Bringing us back to the ideal thing—
There's something fine in a creed like that,
    Something true in those words that ring.
Sneer as you will at the "preacher air,"
    Scoff as you will at the Bible tang,
It's putting God in the Nation's life
    That will keep it clear of the crooked "gang."

We've kept Him out of its life too long,
    We've been afraid—to our utter shame—
To put Him into our speech and song
    To stand on the hustings and speak His name.

We've put all things in that life but Him,
　　We've put our selfishness, pride and show;
It is time for the true ideal to come,
　　And time for the low desire to go.

Putting God in the Nation's life,
　　Helping us think of the higher thing
That is the kind of speech to make
　　That is the kind of song to sing.
Upward and forward and let us try,
　　The new ideal in the forthright way—
Putting God in the Nation's life,
　　And putting it there in a style to stay.

　　　　　　　　　　　　　—Anonymous

GOD REVEALED IN NATURE

God's World

I'm glad I am living this morning,
　　Because the day is so fair,
And I feel God's presence so keenly
　　About me, everywhere.

The heavens declare His glory,
　　The trees seem to speak of His power,
And I see His matchless beauty
　　In each small growing flower.

The rocks all tell of His wonder,
　　In the hills His strength I see;
And the birds are singing His praises
　　In the songs that they sing to me.

I read in the daylight His greatness
　　And the night speaks again of His power;
The raindrops talk of His kindness
　　In each refreshing shower.

Oh, I'm glad to be living this morning,
In a world of beauty so rare
Where the God of Heaven is hovering
About me everywhere.
                              —*Miss Mildred Keeling*
(Used by permission of the Author)

The Nineteenth Psalm

The heavens declare the glory of God;
And the firmament sheweth his handiwork.

Day unto day uttereth speech,
And night unto night sheweth knowledge.

There is no speech nor language;
Their voice cannot be heard.

Their line is gone out through all the earth,
And their words to the end of the world.
In them hath he set a tabernacle for the sun,

Which is as a bridegroom coming out of his chamber,
And rejoiceth as a strong man to run his course.

His going forth is from the end of the heaven,
And his circuit unto the ends of it:
And there is nothing hid from the heat thereof.

The law of the Lord is perfect, restoring the soul:
The testimony of the Lord is sure, making wise the simple.

The precepts of the Lord are right, rejoicing the heart:
The commandment of the Lord is pure, enlightening the
   eyes.

The fear of the Lord is clean, enduring for ever;
The judgments of the Lord are true, and righteous alto-
   gether.

More to be desired are they than gold, yea, than much fine
   gold:
Sweeter also than honey and the honeycomb.

Moreover by them is thy servant warned:
In keeping of them there is great reward.

Who can discern his errors?
Clear thou me from hidden faults.

Keep back thy servant also from presumptuous sins;
Let them not have dominion over me: then shall I be
    perfect,
And I shall be clear from great transgression.

Let the words of my mouth and the meditation of my heart
    be acceptable in thy sight,
O Lord, my rock, and my redeemer.
                    —*The Old Testament. (Eng. Rev. Ver.)*

All Nature Has a Voice to Tell

The God who formed the mountains great
    Can lift the soul to heights sublime;
And He who formed the quiet vales
    Will fill the heart with peace divine.

The One who made the earthly sun
    So full of power and warmth and might,
Can cause the Sun of Righteousness
    To bathe the soul in floods of light.

The boundless ocean e'er proclaims
    A God omnipotent to bless:
The mighty billows are but types
    Of waves divine of righteousness.

As rivers flow to earthly seas
    In deepening, widening, growing power;
So peace which God alone can give
    Grows ever stronger hour by hour.

The treasures hid in earthly caves
    Are only for a fleeting time;
The riches which the Spirit shows
    Are more than rubies, gold, or mine.

The stars of heaven ever tell
Of Christian hopes more bright than they.
The singing birds and beauteous flowers
Proclaim the wisdom of God's way.

All nature has a voice to tell
Of God's great power and love and grace.
His Word and works then let us read
Until we see Him face to face.

—*J. Gilchrist Lawson*

Possession

Heaven above is softer blue
Earth beneath is sweeter green.
Something lives in every hue,
Christless eyes have never seen.
Birds with gladder songs o'erflow,
Flowers with deeper beauty shine
Since I know as now I know
I am His and He is mine.

—*Anonymous*

The Voice of God

You've never heard the voice of God?
Look at the stars above,
Their luminous orbs of many rays,
Speak of infinite love.

The universe to you doth speak
You need not know her laws
The grass the flowers all growing things,
In them there are no flaws.

The seasons as they come and go
The wind, the sun, the rain;
The voice is there and every where,
It speaks and speaks again.

So lift your eyes to the starry sky,
And feel the voice of God.
Oh fainting heart, oh weary soul,
And His great works applaud.
                    —*Katherine R. Barnard*

The Heart's Proof

Do you ask me how I prove
That our Father, God, is love?
By this world which he hath made,
By the songs of grove and blade,
By the brooks that singing run,
By the shining of the sun,
By the breeze that cools my brow,
By fresh odors from the plow,
By the daisy's golden head,
Shining in the fields I tread,
By the chorus of the bees
In the flowering willow trees,
By the gentle dews and rain,
By the farmer's springing grain,
By the light of golden eyes,
By the sheen of forest leaves,
By the sweets of woodland springs,
By the joy right-doing brings—
By a thousand, thousand things!
                    —*James Buckham*

Revelation

All things burn with the fire of God—
Violets bursting from the sod;
The hill-top, tip-toe cherry tree,
Shouting with silver ecstacy;
Wild birds blowing down the wind;
Blue-brook music far and thinned;

Many-hued roses; rains that beat
On spreading fields of yellow wheat;
Sun-flame, moon-flame, flame of star;
Opal-walled heaven where bright clouds are;
Dreams, and pain, and love's desire . . .
All things burn with God's white fire.

—Verne Bright

(Used by permission of the Author)

GOD'S COMING KINGDOM

"God Is Working His Purpose Out"

God is working His purpose out, as year succeeds to year;
God is working His purpose out, and the time is drawing
near.
Nearer and nearer draws the time, the time that shall surely
be,
When the earth shall be filled with the glory of God as the
waters cover the sea.

From utmost east to utmost west, where'er man's foot hath
trod,
By the mouth of many messengers goes forth the voice of
God,
Give ear to me, ye continents; ye isles, give ear to me,
That the earth may be filled with the glory of God as the
waters cover the sea.

What can we do to work God's work, to prosper and in-
crease
The brotherhood of all mankind, the reign of the Prince of
Peace?
What can we do to hasten the time, the time that shall
surely be,
When the earth shall be filled with the glory of God as the
waters cover the sea?

March we forth in the strength of God, with the banner of
    Christ unfurled,
That the light of the glorious Gospel of Truth may shine
    throughout the world;
Fight we the fight with sorrow and sin, to set their captives
    free,
That the earth may be filled with the glory of God as the
    waters cover the sea.

All we can do is nothing worth while, unless God blesses
    the deed;
Vainly we hope for the harvest-tide till God gives life to the
    seed;
Yet nearer and nearer draws the time, the time that shall
    surely be,
When the earth shall be filled with the glory of God as the
    waters cover the sea.

                    —A. C. Ainger

My Father's World

This is my Father's world. O let me ne'er forget
    That tho' the wrong seems oft so strong,
    God is the ruler yet.

This is my Father's world. The battle is not done.
    Jesus who died shall be satisfied,
    And earth and heaven be one.

This is my Father's world. Should my heart be ever sad?
    The Lord is King, let the heavens ring,
    God reigns;—let the earth be glad.

                  —Maltbie D. Babcock

King Triumphant

Jesus shall reign where'er the sun
    Does his successive journeys run;
His kingdom spread from shore to shore,
    Till moons shall wax and wane no more.

From north to south the princes meet,
To pay their homage at his feet;
While western empires own their Lord,
And savage tribes attend his word.

To him shall endless prayer be made,
And endless praises crown his head;
His name, like sweet perfume, shall rise
With ev'ry morning sacrifice.

People and realms of ev'ry tongue
Dwell on his love with sweetest song,
And infant voices shall proclaim
Their early blessings on his name.

—Isaac Watts

Sing Unto Jehovah

Oh sing unto Jehovah a new song;
For he hath done marvellous things:
His right hand, and his holy arm, hath wrought salvation
for him.
Jehovah hath made known his salvation:
His righteousness hath he openly showed in the sight of the
nations.
He hath remembered his loving kindness and his faithful-
ness toward the house of Israel:
All the ends of the earth have seen the salvation of our God.
Make a joyful noise unto Jehovah, all the earth:
Break forth and sing for joy, yea, sing praises.

Sing praises unto Jehovah with the harp;
With the harp and the voice of melody.
With trumpets and sound of cornet
Make a joyful noise before the King, Jehovah.
Let the sea roar, and the fulness thereof;
The world, and they that dwell therein;
Let the floods clap their hands;

Let the hills sing for joy together
Before Jehovah; for he cometh to judge the earth:
He will judge the world with righteousness,
And the peoples with equity.
              —*Psalm 98. (Amer. Stan. Vers.)*

GOD'S LOVE AND CARE FOR US

God's Love

"Yea, I have loved thee with an everlasting love."—Jer. 31:3.

We can only see a little of the ocean,
    A few miles distant from the rocky shore;
But out there—beyond, beyond our eyes' horizon,
    There's more—there's more.

We can only see a little of God's loving—
    A few rich treasures from His mighty store;
But out there—beyond, beyond our eyes' horizon,
    There's more—there's more!
              —*Anonymous*

Walking With God

Sometimes I walk in the shadow,
    Sometimes in sunlight clear;
But whether in gloom or brightness
    The Lord is very near.

Sometimes I walk in the valley,
    Sometimes on the mountain's crest;
But whether on low or high land,
    The Lord is manifest.

Sometimes I walk in the desert,
    Sometimes in waters cold;
But whether by sands or streamlets
    The Lord doth me enfold.

Sometimes I walk in green pastures,
Sometimes on barren land;
But whether in peace or danger,
The Lord holds fast my hand.

—*Anonymous*

God Cares

God cares!
How sweet the strain!
My aching heart and weary brain
Are rested by the sweet refrain,—
He cares, our Father cares!

God cares!
Oh, sing the song
In lonely spot, amid the throng;
'Twill make the way less hard and long,—
He cares, our Father cares!

God cares!
The words so sweet
My lips and life shall e'er repeat,
My burdens all left at His feet,—
God cares, He always cares!

—*Helen Annis Casterline*

Hitherto and Henceforth

"Hitherto hath the Lord helped me."—I. Sam. 7:12.

Hitherto the Lord hath helped us,
Hitherto His hand hath led,
Hitherto His arm protected,
Hitherto His bounty fed;
Will His love desert us wholly,
Will His heart our need forget,
Will His presence clean forsake us,
Who hath never failed us yet?

Still His constant care surrounds us,
Keeping watch by day and night,
And His faithful promise tells us
We are precious in His sight.
He hath set no bounds, no limits,
To His ceaseless gifts of love;
He hath named no times, no seasons,
When His pledge untrue shall prove.

Let the Past we know assure us
Of the Present's certain aid,
Till the Future's dark forebodings
In the light of faith shall fade;
Still He hears our supplications,
As our days our strength shall be;
And His grace is all sufficient
For the needs of you and me.

—Annie Johnson Flint
(Used by permission of the Author)

"My Grace Is Sufficient for Thee"

When, sin-stricken, burdened, and weary,
From bondage I longed to be free,
There came to my heart the sweet message:
"My grace is sufficient for thee."

Though tempted and sadly discouraged,
My soul to this refuge will flee,
And rest in the blessed assurance:
"My grace is sufficient for thee."

My bark may be tossed by the tempest
That sweeps o'er the turbulent sea—
A rainbow illumines the darkness:
"My grace is sufficient for thee."

O Lord, I would press on with courage,
Though rugged the pathway may be,
Sustained and upheld by the promise:
"My grace is sufficient for thee."

Soon, soon will the warfare be over,
My Lord face to face I shall see,
And prove, as I dwell in His presence:
"His grace was sufficient for me."

—*Anonymous*

My Father Knows

This new hymn on God's providence is especially suited to the familiar tune written by George C. Stebbins for Fanny Crosby's hymn, "Saved By Grace," found in many hymnals.

My Father knows my every want;
No help he ever fails to grant,
Whene'er I seek his mind to know,
His will to do, his love to show:
 He knows, he knows, my Father knows,
 And safe his child where'er he goes.

My Father sees my every need,
His watchful eyes scan every deed;
Nor can I wander from his sight
Whose presence fills my life with light:
 He sees, he sees, my Father sees,
 And from all ill his child he frees.

My Father hears my every cry,
His listening ears catch every sigh;
Nor can I call to him in vain
Whose power and love my life sustain:
 He hears, he hears, my Father hears,
 No prayer of faith escapes his ears.

My Father cares, he cares for me,
However low my lot may be;
However great, however small
My burdens be, he cares for all:
 He cares, he cares, my Father cares,
 His children's burdens all he bears.

My Father loves with love so strong,
It fills my heart with grateful song;
Nor life nor death nor depth nor height
Can hide me from his loving sight:
　　He loves, he loves, my Father loves,
　　And safe his child where'er he moves.

My Father knows, my Father hears,
My Father sees, my Father cares,
My Father loves because he knows,
And knowing all, his love o'erflows:
　　He sees, he hears, he cares, he knows;
　　With love for all his heart o'erflows!

　　　　　　　　　—Wilbur Fisk Tillett
　　　　(Used by permission of the Author)

Light Shining Out of Darkness

Thus far the Lord hath led us on—in darkness and in day,
Through all the varied stages of the narrow homeward way.
Long since, he took that journey, he trod that path alone;
Its trials and its dangers full well himself hath known.

Thus far the Lord hath led us—the promise has not failed,
The enemy encountered oft has never quite prevailed;
The shield of faith has turned aside or quenched each fiery
　　dart;
The Spirit's sword in weakest hands has forced him to
　　depart.

Thus far the Lord hath led us—the waters have been high,
But yet in passing through them we felt that he was nigh.
A very present helper in trouble we have found,
His comforts most abounded when our sorrows did abound.

Thus far the Lord hath led us—our need has been supplied,
And mercy has encompassed us about on every side;
Still falls the daily manna, the pure rock-fountains flow,
And many flowers of love and hope along the wayside grow.

Calmly we look behind us, on joys and sorrows past;
We know that all is mercy now, and shall be well at last.
Calmly we look before us—we fear no future ill;
Enough for safety and for peace, if thou art with us still.

Yes, "they that know thy name, O Lord, shall put their
    trust in thee,"
While nothing in themselves but sin and helplessness they
    see.
The race thou hast appointed us, with patience we can run;
Thou wilt perform unto the end the work thou hast begun.
                                    —*Jane Borthwick*

Still, Still With Thee

Still, still with thee, when purple morning breaketh,
    When the bird waketh, and the shadows flee;
Fairer than morning, lovelier than daylight,
    Dawns the sweet consciousness, I am with thee.

Alone with thee, amid the mystic shadows,
    The solemn hush of nature newly born;
Alone with thee in breathless adoration,
    In the calm dew and freshness of the morn.

So shall it be at last, in that bright morning,
    When the soul waketh and life's shadows flee;
O, in that hour, fairer than daylight dawning,
    Shall rise the glorious thought—I am with thee.
                                —*Harriet Beecher Stowe*

Your Father Knoweth

Precious thought, my Father knoweth,
    In His love I rest;
For whate'er my Father doeth
    Must be always best.
Well I know the heart that planneth,
    Nought but good for me;
Joy and sorrow interwoven;
    Love in all I see.

Precious thought, my Father knoweth,
  Careth for His child;
Bids me nestle closer to Him
  When the storm beats wild.
Tho' my earthly hopes are shattered,
  And the tear drops fall,
Yet He is Himself my solace,
  Yea, my Friend, my all.

Oh, to trust Him then more fully,
  Just to simply move
In the conscious, calm enjoyment
  Of the Father's love;
Knowing that life's chequered pathway
  Leadeth to His rest,
Satisfied the way He taketh
  Must be always best.

—*Anonymous*

The Father Knows

Our God and Father surely knows
The evils that so oft oppose
And hinder us along the way.
He knows the trials of each day.

He knows of each corroding care
That crowds our footsteps everywhere;
The burden of each breaking heart
Is known to Him; He bears a part.

Our sorrows and forboding fears,
Our anxious longings and our tears;
Each cherished hope left unfulfilled,
Each heart-cry that has not been stilled—

God knows it all, and cares for me.
He watches o'er me lovingly,
And day by day more precious grows
The knowledge that my Father knows.

My disappointments even may
Be His appointments for this day,
But He will help me with my load
Along life's rough and toilsome road.

Until His love and care are spent
I'll keep my anxious heart content,
For, tho the world may cease to be,
God lives and loves and cares for me.

—F. L. H.

"Daily With You"

"I was daily with you."—Mark 14:49.

He is daily with us, loving, loving, loving,
    Longing to befriend us, waiting but to bless;
Yet we bear our burdens, weary and discouraged,
    And endure our sorrows, lonely, comfortless.

He is daily with us, pleading, pleading, pleading:
    "Come, ye heavy-laden; come to me and rest;"
Yet we struggle onward, tempted, failing, sinning,
    By the hosts of evil beaten and oppressed.

He is daily with us, calling, calling, calling,
    Warning us to follow while we have the Light;
Yet we walk in darkness, sick with doubt and terror,
    And bemoan our stumbling, and bewail the night.

He is daily with us, blessing, breaking, giving,
    Asking but to feed us with the living Bread;
Yet we wander, seeking what earth can not give us,
    Hungering and thirsting, fainting and unfed.

Jesus, daily with us, though we grieve and slight Thee,
    Bear with us yet longer; leave us not, we pray.
Light of God, still leading; love of God, still pleading;
    Christ, still interceding—stay with us to-day!

—Annie Johnson Flint

(Used by permission of the Author)

God Cares

What can it mean? Is it aught to Him
That the nights are long and the days are dim?
Can He be touched by the griefs I bear
Which sadden the heart and whiten the hair?
Around His throne are eternal calms,
And strong, glad music of happy psalms,
And bliss, unruffled by any strife—
How can He care for my little life?

And yet I want Him to care for me,
While I live in this world where the sorrows be;
When the lights die down in the path I take;
When strength is feeble and friends forsake;
When love and music, that once did bless,
Have left me to silence and loneliness,
And my life-song changes to sobbing prayers—
Then my heart cries out for a God who cares.

O, wonderful story of deathless love;
Each child is dear to that heart above;
He fights for me when I cannot fight;
He comforts me in the gloom of night;
He lifts the burden, for He is strong;
He stills the sigh and awakes the song;
The sorrow that bowed me down He bears,
And loves and pardons because He cares.

Let all who are sad take heart again,
We are not alone in our hours of pain;
Our Father stoops from His throne above
To soothe and quiet us with His love.
He leaves us not when the storm is high,
And we have safety, for He is nigh.
Can it be trouble which He doth share?
O, rest in peace, for the Lord doth care.

—*Marianne Farningham*

The Love of the Father

It comes to me more and more,
  Each day as I pass along,
The love of the Father eternal
  Is over us tender and strong.

'Tis not alone in the sunshine
  Our lives grow pure and true;
There is growth as well in the shadow,
  And pain has a work to do.

A message comes in the heartache,
  A whisper of love in the pain;
The pangs we have fought and conquered
  Tell the sweet story of gain.

So it comes to me more and more
  As I enter upon each new day;
The love of the Father eternal
  Is over us all the way.

—*Anonymous*

God the Omniscient

There is an Eye that never sleeps
  Beneath the wing of night;
There is an Ear that never shuts
  When sink the beams of light.
There is an Arm that never tires
  When human strength gives way;
There is a Love that never fails
  When earthly loves decay.
That Eye unseen o'erwatcheth all;
  That Arm upholds the sky;
That Ear doth hear the sparrow's call;
  That Love is ever nigh.

—*James Cowden Wallace*

Contentment

Behold the ravens on the trees,
  They neither sow nor reap,
Nor do they gather into barns
  Store for their winter's keep.
Yet every one thy Father feeds,
  And should He pass thee by?
Does He not know His children's needs,
  Nor heed them when they cry?

Behold the lilies as they grow,
  They neither toil nor spin,
Yet human ne'er wore robes as fine
  As God hath clothed them in.
Could He, who clothes the fragile flow'r,
  Forget to clothe His own?
In faith lay hold upon His pow'r,
  To Him thy cares make known!

Seek not what ye shall drink or eat,
  Nor be of "doubtful mind,"
Such is a hopeless world's conceit,
  Ye have a Father kind!
Seek ye the Kingdom of the Lord
  And seek His righteousness:
With all good things, so says His Word,
  Will He His children bless.

—Benjamin Schlipf

The Everlasting Love

"Jesus . . . having loved his own . . . loved them unto the end."
—John 13:1.

Though we may waver, He remaineth steadfast,
  And all his words are sure;
From everlasting unto everlasting
  His promises endure.

Though we may wander, He will not forsake us,
    Truer than earthly friend;
He never fails our trust, for having loved us,
    He loves unto the end.

Unto the end; we doubt Him, we deny Him,
    We wound Him, we forget;
We set some earthly idol up between us
    Without one faint regret.

And when it falls or crumbles, and in anguish
    We seek this changeless Friend,
Lo! He receives us, comforts and forgives us,
    And loves us to the end.

—*Annie Johnson Flint*
(Used by permission of the Author)

More Than We Ask

I asked for just a crumb of bread.
Within His banquet-hall he spread
A bounteous feast on every side—
My hungry soul was satisfied.

I asked for just a ray of light
To guide me through the gloomy night,
And lo, there shone along my way
The noon-tide glory of the day.

I asked for just a little aid,
As I stood trembling and afraid.
With strength I had not known before
He made me more than conqueror.

I asked for just a bit of love,
For love is sweet. From heaven above
The words came now with meaning new,
"Upon the Cross I died for you."

—*Faith Wells*

Just the Same To-day

When Moses and his people
From Egypt's land did flee,
Their enemies behind them,
And in front of them the sea,
God raised the waters like a wall
And opened up the way,
And the God that lived in Moses' time
Is just the same to-day.

When David and Goliath met,
The wrong against the right—
The giant armed with human power
And David with God's might;
God's power with David's sling and stone
The giant low did lay,
And the God that lived in David's time
Is just the same to-day.

When Pentecost had fully come,
And the fire from Heaven did fall,
As a mighty wind the Holy Ghost
Baptized them one and all;
Three thousand got converted,
And were workers right away
And the God that lived at Pentecost,
Is just the same to-day.

—*Anonymous*

A Business Man's Prayer

Dear Lord, I do not hesitate
To thank Thee for things truly great;
The universe is Thine, and all
Accomplishment is at Thy call.
Lord of each mountain art Thou, still—
Art Thou of each little hill.

It pleases me to know I may
Receive Thy backing every day
In all the larger things of life,
Howe'er gigantic be the strife;
But this thought pleases best of all—
Lord art Thou of the very small.

No matter how great be my goal,
'Tis little tasks make up the whole,
And the sure knowledge that Thou art
The Lord of each gives to my heart
The strength to face them one by one
Until the larger task is done.

When 'tis completed, I agree
The finished product's due to Thee;
I thank Thee for it as a whole,
But deep down in my toiling soul
My gratitude the greater clings
To Thee as Lord of little things.

—*William Ludlum*

(Used by permission of the Author)

Faith and Sight

Our eyes are holden that we do not see
How patiently He stands, how lovingly,
The while we pause, affrighted at the way,
Ere we have crossed the threshold of the day.
The fulness of the joy He'd have us know
Ofttimes we miss, because we are so slow
To trust him, even when we hear him say,
"Fear not; lo, I am with you all the way."
Sometimes He lifts the veil and lets us see
How close beside He stands to you and me.
Ah! then we know it is his hand, his touch,
Moves this and that, that hinders overmuch,
And learn, at last, unfalt'ringly to say,
I know He will abide with me to-day.

—*Anna M. King*

And Yet—

To think of it! He knows me
　　Through and through;
And yet He loves me,
　　Tenderly and true.

—Arthur B. Rhinow

God Provides

Behold
The birds
　　Of the heaven,
That they sow not,
　　Neither do they reap,
Nor gather
　　Into barns;
And your heavenly Father
　　Feedeth them.

Are not ye
　　Of much more
Value than they?
　　And which of you
By being anxious
　　Can add one cubit
Unto the measure
　　Of his life?

And why
　　Are ye anxious
Concerning raiment?
　　Consider the lilies
Of the field,
　　How they grow;
They toil not,
　　Neither do they spin:

Yet I say unto you,
That even Solomon
In all his glory
Was not arrayed
Like one of these.
New Testament (Amer. Stand. Ver.)

Divine Abundance

The grasses are clothed
And the ravens are fed
    From His store;
But you, who are loved
And guarded and led,
    How much more
Will He clothe and feed you and give you His care?
Then leave it with Him; He has everywhere
    Ample store.

—Anonymous

Eternal Goodness

I know not what the future hath
    Of marvel or surprise,
Assured alone that life and death,
    His mercy underlies:

And so beside the Silent Sea
    I wait the muffled oar;
No harm from Him can come to me
    On ocean or on shore.

I know not where His islands lift
    Their fronded palms in air;
I only know I cannot drift
    Beyond His love and care.

—John Greenleaf Whittier

The Work of Love

It was Love that built the mountains,
　It was Love that made the sea—
It was Love that put all beauty
　In the world, for you and me.
It was Love that gave us flowers,
　It was Love that gave us tears,
It was Love that lent us laughter
　To make gay the lonely years!

It was Love that gave us friendship,
　It was Love that offered peace—
Oh, Love can bring to suffering,
　A splendid, swift release!
It was Love that planted happiness
　Wherever hearts are found—
Oh, it's Love, Love, Love, LOVE,
　That makes the world go 'round!

　　　　　　　　　　—Margaret Sangster

(Used by permission of the Author)

GOD'S WILLINGNESS TO SAVE

Compel Them To Come In

"Go ye into the highways
　And to the hedges go!"
So said the Master to His Church
　Two thousand years ago.

Go, seek the lowly and the poor,
　The outcast slaves of sin;
So far from closing mercy's door,
　"Compel them to come in!"

Why, then? The Master's feast is spread,
So wide His love and care;
His heavenly bounty, rich and free,
He would have all to share.

The door of God is never closed
To any needy soul.
Men may be down, but never out
With Him who loveth all.

"Compel them to come in!" His voice
Peals through the centuries old.
Let Love Divine through human hearts
Compel them to the fold.

—*Leonard Dodd*

GUIDANCE

This Moment

"A very present help."—Psalms 46:1.

He's helping me now—this moment,
Though I may not see it or hear,
Perhaps by a friend far distant,
Perhaps by a stranger near,
Perhaps by a spoken message,
Perhaps by the printed word;
In ways that I know and know not,
I have the help of the Lord.

He's keeping me now—this moment,
However I need it most,
Perhaps by a single angel,
Perhaps by a mighty host,
Perhaps by the chain that frets me,
Or the walls that shut me in;
In ways that I know and know not,
He keeps me from harm or sin.

He's guiding me now—this moment,
   In pathways easy or hard,
Perhaps by a door wide open,
   Perhaps by a door fast barred,
Perhaps by a joy withholden,
   Perhaps by a gladness given;
In ways that I know and know not,
   He's leading me up to heaven.

He's using me now—this moment,
   And whether I go or stand,
Perhaps by a plan accomplished,
   Perhaps when He stays my hand,
Perhaps by a word in season,
   Perhaps by a silent prayer;
In ways that I know and know not,
   His labor of love I share.

                    —*Annie Johnson Flint*
         (Used by permission of the Author)

God Is In Every Tomorrow

God is in every tomorrow,
   Therefore I live for today,
Certain of finding at sunrise,
   Guidance and strength for the way;
Power for each moment of weakness,
   Hope for each moment of pain,
Comfort for every sorrow,
   Sunshine and joy after rain.

God is in every tomorrow,
   Planning for you and for me;
E'en in the dark will I follow,
   Trust where my eyes cannot see.
Stilled by His promise of blessing,
   Soothed by the touch of His hand,
Confident in His protection,
   Knowing my life-path is planned.

God is in every tomorrow,
    Life with its changes may come,
He is behind and before me,
    While in the distance shines home!
Home—where no thought of tomorrow
    Ever can shadow my brow,
Home—in the presence of Jesus,
    Through all eternity—now!
            —*Laura A. Barter Snow,* in *"With Tongue and Pen"*

What God Hath Promised!

God hath not promised
    Skies always blue,
Flower-strewn pathways
    All our lives through;
God hath not promised
    Sun without rain,
Joy without sorrow,
    Peace without pain.

But God hath promised
    Strength for the day,
Rest for the labor,
    Light for the way,
Grace for the trials,
    Help from above,
Unfailing sympathy,
    Undying Love.
            —*Annie Johnson Flint*
(Used by permission of the Author)

He Leadeth Me

He leadeth me! O blessed thought!
O words with heavenly comfort fraught!
Whate'er I do, where'er I be,
Still 'tis God's hand that leadeth me.

He leadeth me, he leadeth me,
By his own hand he leadeth me:
His faithful follower I would be,
For by his hand he leadeth me.

Sometimes 'mid scenes of deepest gloom,
Sometimes where Eden's bowers bloom,
By waters still, o'er troubled sea,
Still 'tis his hand that leadeth me!

Lord, I would clasp thy hand in mine,
Nor ever murmur nor repine,
Content, whatever lot I see,
Since 'tis my God that leadeth me!

—Joseph H. Gilmore

Jesus and I

I can not do it alone;
    The waves run fast and high,
And the fogs close chill around,
    And the light goes out in the sky;
But I know that we two shall win in the end—
    Jesus and I.

I can not row it myself,
    My boat on the raging sea;
But beside me sits Another,
    Who pulls or steers with me;
And I know that we too shall come into port—
    His child and He.

Coward and wayward and weak,
    I change with the changing sky,
To-day so eager and brave,
    To-morrow not caring to try;
But He never gives in, so we two shall win—
    Jesus and I.

Strong and tender and true,
  Crucified once for me;
Never will He change, I know,
  Whatever I may be;
But all He says I must do,
  Ever from sin to keep free.
We shall finish our course and reach home at last—
  His child and He.

—*Dan Crawford*

Resurgam

Backward we look regretful, forward we glance with dread;
If God be not our refuge, hope in the dust lies dead.
Backward we glance with praises, forward we look with
    cheer,
God is our strength and portion, fearless we face the year.

We went through fire and water, but the Lord God brought
    us out,
With gladness and rejoicing and a triumphant shout.
Upon our backs were furrows, the foe plowed deep and sore;
His pity wrought deliverance, praise him for evermore.

Life's desert way was dreary, o'erhead the fierce sun beat,
He was comfort and refreshment and a refuge from the
    heat.
The torrents drove upon us, we watched the storm-clouds
    form,
But God rode on the tempest, he was shelter in the storm.

Bondage had seared our spirits, sin's shame was on our face,
When Love redeemed and set us in a spacious, wealthy
    place.
Now light is on our pathway, gone is our faithless care;
Blessed be God, who bides in grace and turns not from our
    prayer.

—*W. Nelson Bitton*

Disappointment—His Appointment

"He performeth the thing that is appointed for me."—Job 23:14.

"Disappointment—His *appointment*,"
  Change one letter, then I see
That the thwarting of my purpose
  Is God's better choice for me.
His appointment must be blessing,
  Tho' it may come in disguise,
For the end from the beginning
  Open to His wisdom lies.

"Disappointment—His *appointment*,"
  Whose? The Lord, who loves me best,
Understands and knows me fully,
  Who my faith and love would test;
For, like loving earthly parent,
  He rejoices when He knows
That His child accepts, UNQUESTIONED,
  All that from His wisdom flows.

"Disappointment—His *appointment*,"
  "No good thing will He withhold,"
From denials oft we gather
  Treasures of His love untold.
Well He knows each broken purpose
  Leads to fuller, deeper trust,
And the end of all His dealings
  Proves our God is wise and just.

"Disappointment—His *appointment*,"
  Lord, I take it, then, as such.
Like the clay in hands of potter,
  Yielding wholly to Thy touch.
All my life's plan is Thy moulding,
  Not one single choice be mine;
Let me answer, unrepining—
  Father, "Not my will, but Thine."

                    —*Edith Lillian Young*

The Mosaic Worker

Patient above his tinted tiles he bent
With certain touch as if he knew
The meaning in the glinting disarray
Would find at last a pattern true.

And slowly beauty flowered at his will
Telling the beauty hidden in his thought,
With fragments, broken, shapeless, each in place
Until the perfect whole he wrought.

So may our days, unmeaning each by each,
Fragmentary, patternless, and dull
Under the Craftsman's sure and knowing hand
Become a life made beautiful!

—*Arthur Wallace Peach*

Abide With Me

Abide with me: fast falls the eventide;
The darkness deepens; Lord, with me abide:
When other helpers fail, and comforts flee,
Help of the helpless, oh, abide with me!

Swift to its close ebbs out life's little day;
Earth's joys grow dim, its glories pass away;
Change and decay in all around I see:
O Thou Who changeth not, abide with me!

I need Thy presence every passing hour:
What but Thy grace can foil the tempter's pow'r?
Who like Thyself my guide and stay can be?
Through cloud and sunshine, oh, abide with me!

I fear no foe with Thee at hand to bless;
Ills have no weight, and tears no bitterness;
Where is death's sting? where, grave, thy victory?
I triumph still, if Thou abide with me.

Hold Thou Thy cross before my closing eyes;
Shine through the gloom, and point me to the skies.
Heaven's morning breaks, and earth's vain shadows flee—
In life, in death, O Lord, abide with me!
                                        —*Henry F. Lyte*

Leave the Thread With God

Spin cheerfully,
Not tearfully,
Though wearily you plod.
Spin carefully,
Spin prayerfully,
But leave the thread to God.

The shuttles of His purpose move
To carry out His own design,
Seek not too soon to disapprove
His work, nor yet assign
Dark motives, when with silent dread
You view each sombre fold,
For lo! within each darker thread
There shines a thread of gold.

Spin cheerfully,
Not tearfully,
He knows the way you plod;
Spin carefully,
Spin prayerfully,
But leave the thread with God.
                                        —*Anonymous*

Our Father's Hand

In a factory building there are wheels and gearings,
There are cranks and pulleys, beltings tight or slack,—
Some are whirling swiftly, some are turning slowly,
Some are thrusting forward, some are pulling back;
Some are smooth and silent, some are rough and noisy,
Pounding, rattling, clanking, moving with a jerk;

In a wild confusion in a seeming chaos,
Lifting, pushing, driving,—but they do their work,
From the mightiest lever to the tiniest pinion,
All things move together for the purpose planned;
And behind the working is a mind controlling,
And a force directing, and a guiding hand.

So all things are working for the Lord's beloved;
Some things might be hurtful if alone they stood;
Some might seem to hinder, some might draw us backward;
But they work together, and they work for good,
All the thwarted longings, all the stern denials,
All the contradictions, hard to understand,
And the force that holds them, speeds them and retards
    them
Stops and starts and guides them,—is our Father's hand.
                  —Annie Johnson Flint
(Used by permission of the Author)

Life and the Weaver

Life is a woven fabric;
    The pattern and web are wrought
By the dark threads and the golden
    That into the loom are shot.

You cannot judge God's purpose
    By the thrust of a single thread,
What to you may be dark, mysterious,
    May be gloriously bright instead.

For He holds in mind a pattern
    As fair as His love is strong,
Which grows each day in the weaving;
    Not a single thread goes wrong.

No warp in His hands shall tangle,
    No slumber His eyelids close;
We only can thwart His purpose
    When our stubborn wills impose.

Our tangled and broken efforts
   To walk in His kind commands
Will give life an added luster,
   Restored by His loving hands.

So trust in the Weaver's wisdom,
   In His love and unfailing care,
And the fabric of life, completed,
   Some day will be wondrous fair.

—A. W. Dewar

Through the Maze

He leads us on
Through all the unquiet years;
Past all our dreamland hopes, and doubts, and fears
He guides our steps. Through all the tangled maze
Of sin, of sorrow, and o'erclouded days
   We know His will is done,
   And still He leads us on.

—Anonymous

Jesus, Saviour, Pilot Me

Jesus, Saviour, pilot me,
Over life's tempestuous sea;
Unknown waves before me roll,
Hiding rock and treacherous shoal:
Chart and compass come from Thee:
Jesus, Saviour, pilot me.

As a mother stills her child,
Thou canst hush the ocean wild;
Boisterous waves obey Thy will
When thou say'st to them "Be still!"
Wondrous Sovereign of the sea,
Jesus, Saviour, pilot me.

When at last I near the shore,
And the fearful breakers roar
'Twixt me and the peaceful rest,
Then, while leaning on Thy breast,
May I hear Thee say to me,
"Fear not, I will pilot thee!"
—*Rev. Edward Hopper*

The Unerring Guide

I have a proved, unerring Guide,
  Whose love I'm loth to grieve;
He brings me golden promises
  My heart can scarce receive;
He leadeth me, and hope and cheer
  Doth for my path provide,
For dreary nights and days of drought:
  Have you so sure a Guide?
Quench not the faintest whisper
  That the heavenly dove may bring;
He seeks with holy love to lure
  The wanderer 'neath His wing.
—*Anna Shipton*

The Tapestry Weavers

Let us take to our hearts a lesson—no lesson can braver
    be—
From the ways of the tapestry weavers on the other side of
    the sea.
Above their heads the pattern hangs, they study it with
    care,
And while their fingers deftly work, their eyes are fastened
    there.
They tell this curious thing, besides, of the patient, plod-
    ding weaver;
He works on the wrong side evermore, but works for the
    right side ever.

It is only when the weaving stops, and the web is tossed
and turned,
And he sees his real handiwork, that his marvelous skill is
learned.
Ah, the sight of its delicate beauty, how it pays him for all
it cost,
No rarer, daintier work than his was ever done by the frost.
Thus the master bringeth him golden hire and giveth him
praises as well,
And how happy the heart of the weaver is, no tongue but
his own can tell.

The years of man are the looms of God let down from the
place of the sun,
Wherein we are weaving always, till the mystic web is done.
Weaving kindly; but weaving surely, each for himself, his
fate,
We may not see how the right side looks, we can only weave
and wait.
But looking above for the pattern, no weaver hath need to
fear,
Only let him look clear into heaven—the perfect pattern is
there.

If he keeps the face of the Saviour forever and always in
sight,
His toil shall be sweeter than honey, his weaving is sure to
be right.
And when his task is ended, and the web is turned and
shown,
He shall hear the voice of the Master, it shall say to him,
"Well done!"
And the white-winged angels of heaven to bear him thence
shall come down,
And God shall give him gold for his hire, not coin, but a
fadeless crown.

—Anson G. Chester, D.D.

To the End

O Jesus, I have promised
    To serve Thee to the end;
Be Thou forever near me,
    My Master and my Friend;
I shall not fear the battle
    If Thou art by my side,
Nor wander from the pathway
    If Thou wilt be my Guide.

—John E. Bode

God's Plans

He will silently plan for thee;
His purposes shall all unfold.
The tangled skein shall shine at last,
A masterpiece of skill untold.

He will silently plan for thee,
Happy child of a Father's care,
As though no other claimed His love,
But thou alone to Him wert dear.

—Anonymous

The Divine Hand

Guide me, O Thou great Jehovah,
    Pilgrim through this barren land;
I am weak, but Thou art mighty;
    Hold me with Thy powerful hand;
Bread of heaven!   Bread of heaven,
    Feed me till I want no more.

—William Williams

HEART—PURITY

Purity of Heart

Blest are the pure in heart,
  For they shall see our God;
The secret of the Lord is theirs;
  Their soul is His abode.

Still to the lowly soul
  He doth himself impart,
And for His service and his throne
  Selects the pure in heart.

—John Keble

HEAVEN

Sequence

After the sea, the harbor;
  After the storm, the calm;
After the road, the arbor;
  After the bleeding, balm;
After the gladness, weeping;
  After the bloom, the clod;
After the labor, sleeping;
  After the sleeping—God!

—Edgar Daniel Kramer

God's Trails Lead Home

"All the trails of God lead home."—John J. Lawrence, D.D.

God's trails lead home,
  To home beyond the blue,
To yon fair land
  Where all is real and true.

God's trails lead home,
  The home of endless day,
The land of peace
  Whose sun shines on for aye.

God's trails lead home
  To where our loved ones dwell,
Where Jesus reigns
  And heavenly anthems swell.

God's trails lead home,
  The home of timeless years,
The land of love,
  Where all unknown are tears.
                    —*John R. Clements*

The King's Highway

A wonderful way is the King's Highway;
It runs through the nightland up to the Day;
From the wonderful WAS, by the wonderful IS,
To the still more wonderful IS TO BE
  —Runs the King's Highway.
                    —*John Masefield*
          (Used by permission of the Author)

Home of the Soul

I will sing you a song of that beautiful land,
  The far-away home of the soul,
Where no storms ever beat on the glittering strand,
  While the years of eternity roll.

Oh, that home of the soul in my visions and dreams,
  Its bright, jasper walls I can see;
Till I fancy but thinly the veil intervenes
  Between that fair city and me.

That unchangeable home is for you and for me,
    Where Jesus of Nazareth stands,
The King of all kingdoms forever is he,
    And he holdeth our crowns in his hands.

Oh, how sweet it will be in that beautiful land,
    So free from all sorrow and pain;
With songs on our lips and with harps in our hands,
    To meet one another again.

                              —*Ellen H. Gates*

The Homeland

The Homeland! Oh, the Homeland!
    The land of the freeborn!
There's no night in the Homeland
    But aye the fadeless morn;
I'm sighing for the Homeland,
    My heart is aching here;
There is no pain in the Homeland
    To which I'm drawing near.

My Lord is in the Homeland,
    With angels bright and fair;
There's no sin in the Homeland,
    And no temptation there;
The music of the Homeland
    Is ringing in my ears,
And when I think of the Homeland,
    My eyes are filled with tears.

My loved ones in the Homeland
    Are waiting me to come
Where neither death nor sorrow
    Invades their holy home:
O dear, dear native Country!
    O rest and peace above!
Christ bring us all to the Homeland
    Of His eternal love.

                    —*Hugh Reginald Haweis*

The End of the Way

Written by Miss Harriet Cole of Milton, Nova Scotia, who was bedridden for many years.

My life is a wearisome journey;
  I'm sick with the dust and the heat;
The rays of the sun beat upon me;
  The briers are wounding my feet;
But the city to which I am going
  Will more than my trials repay;
All the toils of the road will seem nothing
  When I get to the end of the way.

There are so many hills to climb upward
  I often am longing for rest;
But He who appoints me my pathway
  Knows just what is needful and best;
I know in His word He has promised
  That my strength shall be as my day;
And the toils of the road will seem nothing
  When I get to the end of the way.

He loves me too well to forsake me
  Or give me one trial too much;
All His people have been dearly purchased,
  And Satan can never claim such.
By and by I shall see Him and praise Him
  In the city of unending day;
And the toils of the road will seem nothing
  When I get to the end of the way.

Though now I am footsore and weary,
  I shall rest when I'm safely at home.
I know I'll receive a glad welcome,
  For the Saviour Himself has said, "Come."
So when I am weary in body
  And sinking in spirit, I say,
"All the toils of the road will seem nothing
  When I get to the end of the way."

When the last feeble step has been taken,
　And the gates of the city appear,
And the beautiful songs of the angels
　Float out on my listening ear;
Then all that now seems so mysterious
　Will be plain and clear as the day,
Yes, the toils of the road will seem nothing
　When I get to the end of the way.

Cooling fountains are there for the thirsty;
　There are cordials for those who are faint;
There are robes that are whiter and purer
　Then any that fancy can paint;
Then I'll try to press hopefully onward,
　Thinking often through each weary day,
"The toils of the road will seem nothing
　When I get to the end of the way."

—Harriet Cole

Waiting for the Dawning

I am waiting for the dawning
　Of the bright and blessed day;
When the darksome night of sorrow
　Shall have vanished far away:
When forever with the Saviour,
　Far beyond this vale of tears,
I shall swell the song of worship
　Through the everlasting years.

I am looking at the brightness,
　(See, it shineth from afar),
Of the clear and joyous beaming,
　Of the "Bright and Morning Star,"
Through the dark grey mist of morning
　Do I see its glorious light;
Then away with every shadow
　Of this sad and weary night.

I am waiting for the coming
　Of the Lord who died for me:
Oh, His words have thrilled my spirit,
　"I will come again for thee."
I can almost hear His footfall
　On the threshold of the door,
And my heart, my heart is longing
　To be His for evermore.

—Anonymous

Nearer Home

One sweetly solemn thought
　Comes to me o'er and o'er:
I am nearer my home to-day
　Than I ever have been before;

Nearer my Father's house,
　Where the many mansions be;
Nearer the great white throne,
　Nearer the crystal sea;

Nearer the bound of life,
　Where we lay our burden down;
Nearer leaving the cross;
　Nearer gaining the crown:

But lying darkly between,
　Winding down through the night,
Is the silent, unknown stream,
　That leads at last to the light.

Closer and closer my steps
　Come to the dark abysm;
Closer Death to my lips
　Presses the awful chrism.

Oh, if my mortal feet
　Have almost gained the brink;
If it be I am nearer home
　Even to-day than I think!

Father, perfect my trust;
Let my spirit feel in death,
That her feet are firmly set
On the rock of a living faith!

—*Phœbe Cary*

The Holy City

Last night I lay a-sleeping,
There came a dream so fair;
I stood in old Jerusalem,
Beside the Temple there;
I heard the children singing,
And ever as they sang,
Methought the voice of angels
From heaven in answer rang,
  Jerusalem, Jerusalem,
  Lift up your gates and sing
  Hosanna in the highest,
  Hosanna to your King!

And then methought my dream was changed,
The streets no longer rang,
Hushed were the glad Hosannas
The little children sang;
The sun grew dark with mystery,
The morn was cold and chill,
As the shadow of a cross arose
Upon a lonely hill.
  Jerusalem, Jerusalem,
  Hark! how the angels sing,
  Hosanna in the highest,
  Hosanna to your King!

And once again the scene was changed,
New earth there seemed to be!
I saw the holy city
Beside the tideless sea;

The light of God was on its street,
The gates were open wide;
And all who would might enter,
And no one was denied.
No need of moon or stars by night,
Nor sun to shine by day;
It was the New Jerusalem,
That would not pass away.
   Jerusalem, Jerusalem,
   Sing, for the night is o'er,
   Hosanna in the highest,
   Hosanna for evermore!

—F. E. Weatherly

HUMILITY

Enough!

He that is down needs fear no fall,
   He that is low, no pride;
He that is humble ever shall
   Have God to be his guide.

I am content with that I have,
   Little be it or much;
And Lord, contentment still I crave,
   Because thou savest such.

Fullness to such a burden is
   That go on pilgrimage;
Here little, and hereafter bliss,
   Is best from age to age.

—John Bunyan

HYMNS

The Old Hymns

There's a lot of music in 'em—the hymns of long ago,
And when some gray-haired brother sings the ones I used to
  know
I sorter want to take his hand—I think of days gone by—
"On Jordan's story banks I stand and cast a wistful eye!"

There's lots of music in 'em—those dear sweet hymns of
  old,
With visions bright of lands of light and shining streets of
  gold;
And hear 'em—singing where Memory dreaming stands,
"From Greenland's icy mountains to India's coral strands."

They seem to sing forever of holier, sweeter days,
When the lilies of the love of God bloomed white in all the
  ways,
And I want to hear their music from the old-time meetings
  rise
Till "I can read my title clear to mansions in the skies."

We never needed singin' books in them old days—we knew
The words, the tunes of every one—the dear old hymn book
  through!
We didn't have no trumpets then, no organs built for show,
We only sang to praise the Lord, "from whom all blessings
  flow."

And so I love the old hymns and when my time shall
  come—
Before the light has left me, and my singing lips are dumb—
If I can hear 'em sing them then, I'll pass without a sigh
To "Canaan's fair and happy land, where my possessions
  lie."

—Frank L. Stanton, in *The Atlanta Constitution*

LABOR

A Little Song of Work

Elijah's mantle fell upon
  Elisha plowing sod;
And Gideon was threshing wheat
  When he was called of God.

To Moses and to David came
  The call when shepherding;
For labor so befits a man
  And dignifies a king.

One day the Holy Ghost, elect
  Of God triune to choose
Ambassadors, poured holy oil
  On Moody—selling shoes!

The Saviour was a carpenter;
  The Roman's nails crashed through
Fine, manly hands that callouses
  Of homely labor knew.

And Paul, Apostle, like his Lord,
  Had learned a trade and stands
An honor to the working-man
  Who serves with honest hands.

And so, with greater gifts of grace,
  O Soul, name thou to bless
The gift of work; its fellowship
  And rugged fruitfulness.
                    —Sarah Elizabeth Sprouse

LIVING FOR GOD

The Gospel According To You

There's a sweet old story translated for man,
  But writ in the long, long ago—
The Gospel according to Mark, Luke and John—
  Of Christ and his mission below.

Men read and admire the Gospel of Christ,
  With its love so unfailing and true;
But what do they say, and what do they think,
  Of the gospel "according to you?"

'Tis a wonderful story, that gospel of love,
  As it shines in the Christ life divine;
And, oh, that its truth might be told again
  In the story of your life and mine!

Unselfishness mirrors in every scene;
  Love blossoms on every sod;
And back from its vision the heart comes to tell
  The wonderful goodness of God.

You are writing each day a letter to men;
  Take care that the writing is true;
'Tis the only gospel that some men will read—
  That gospel according to you.

—*Anonymous*

The One Thing Needful

Some seek for ecstasies of joy;
  Others for gifts of power,
That they might work great miracles,
  As prophets did of yore.
But as for me, one thing I ask:
Grace to perform my daily task.

Some fain would know all mysteries,
  Would open every door
That leads into the vast unknown,
  Its secrets to explore.
I'd rather have a heart made clean
To see my God with nought between.

If I could heap up treasured store
  From every foreign strand,
And all the prizes of success
  Retain within my hand,—
Unless my Father's smile I know,
I'm still a pauper here below.

—*Max Isaac Reich*

(Used by permission of the Author)

Your Own Version

You are writing a gospel,
  A chapter each day,
By deeds that you do,
  By words that you say.

Men read what you write,
  Whether faithless or true;
Say, what is the gospel
  According to you?

—*Paul Gilbert*

Live Christ

Live Christ!—and though thy way may be
  In this world's sight adversity,
He who doth heed thine every need
  Shall give thy soul prosperity.

Live Christ!—and though thy path may be
  The narrow street of poverty,
He had not where to lay his head,
  Yet lived in largest liberty.

Live Christ!—and though thy life may be
   The straight way of humility,
He who first trod that way of God
   Will clothe thee with His dignity.

Live Christ!—and though thy life may be
   In much a valedictory,
The heavy cross brings seeming loss,
   But wins the crown of victory.

Live Christ!—and all thy life shall be
   A highway of delivery—
A royal road of goodly deeds,
   Gold-paved with sweetest charity.

Live Christ!—and all thy life shall be
   A sweet, uplifting ministry,
A sowing of the fair white seeds
   That fruit through all eternity.

—*John Oxenham*

(Used by permission of the Author)

Take Time To Be Holy

Take time to be holy;
   Speak oft with thy Lord;
Abide in Him always
   And feed on His word.
Make friends of God's children,
   Help those who are weak,
Forgetting in nothing
   His blessing to seek.

Take time to be holy;
   The world rushes on;
Spend much time in secret
   With Jesus alone.
By looking to Jesus,
   Like Him thou shalt be;
Thy friends in thy conduct
   His likeness shall see.

Take time to be holy;
  Let Him be thy Guide,
And run not before Him
  Whatever betide.
In joy or in sorrow
  Still follow thy Lord
And, looking to Jesus,
  Still trust in His word.

—*W. D. Longstaff*

Pass It On

Have you had a kindness shown?
  Pass it on;
'Twas not given for thee alone,
  Pass it on;
Let it travel down the years,
Let it wipe another's tears,
Till in heaven the deed appears—
  Pass it on.

Did you hear a loving word?
  Pass it on;
Like the singing of a bird?
  Pass it on;
Let its music live and grow,
Let it cheer another's woe,
You have reap'd what others sow—
  Pass it on.

Be not selfish in thy greed,
  Pass it on;
Look upon thy brother's need,
  Pass it on;
Live for self, you live in vain,
Live for Christ, you live again,
Live for Him, with Him you reign—
  Pass it on.

—*Henry K. Burton*

I Shall Not Pass Again This Way

The bread that giveth strength I want to give;
The water pure that bids the thirsty live;
I want to help the fainting day by day,
Because I shall not pass again this way.

I want to give the oil of joy for tears;
The faith to conquer cruel doubts and fears;
Beauty for ashes may I give alway,
Because I shall not pass again this way.

I want to give good measure running o'er,
And into angry hearts I want to pour
The answer soft that turneth wrath away,
Because I shall not pass again this way.

I want to give to others hope and faith;
I want to do all that the Master saith;
I want to live aright from day to day,
Because I shall not pass again this way.

—Anonymous

The Challenge

The challenge comes
    To Christian men;
The world demands
    New proof again.

Material might,
    With ugly mien,
Defies the power
    Of things unseen.

The church, the Book,
    Must stand the test,
To show the world
    God's truth is best.

The cause of Christ
    Must suffer loss
If Christian men
    Bear not the cross.

No longer words
    Nor empty creeds;
The world demands
    New proof in deeds.
                        —*Grenville Kleiser*

A Prayer

Those who love Thee may they find,
Thou for evermore art kind;
Those who trust Thee may they know,
Thou dost hear their cry below.

Those who serve Thee may they see,
Service draws them near to Thee!
May this service, trust and love,
Lead at last to heaven above!
                        —*George F. Chawner*

God Wants a Man

God wants a man—honest and true and brave;
    A man who hates the wrong and loves the right;
A man who scorns all compromise with sin,
    Who for the truth courageously will fight.

God wants a man—in lowly walk or high,
    Who to the world by daily life will prove
That Christ abides within the yielded heart,
    Fitting that heart for service and for love.

God wants a man who dares to tell the truth,
    Who in the market-place will stand four-square;
Whose word men trust—a man who never stoops
    To hurt his fellow or to act unfair.

God wants a man of action and of faith,
  Whose life is something more than cant and talk;
Who lives each day as though it were his last,
  And proves his faith by a consistent walk.

—Anonymous

The Harder Task

Teach me to live! 'Tis easier far to die—
  Gently and silently to pass away—
On earth's long night to close the heavy eye,
  And waken in the glorious realms of day.

Teach me that harder lesson—how to live
  To serve Thee in the darkest paths of life.
Arm me for conflict, now fresh vigor give,
  And make me more than conqu'ror in the strife.

—Anonymous

Something For Jesus

Saviour! Thy dying love
Thou gavest me,
Nor should I ought withhold,
Dear Lord, from Thee;
In love my soul would bow,
My heart fulfil its vow,
Some offering bring Thee now,
Something for Thee.

Give me a faithful heart—
Likeness to Thee—
That each departing day
Henceforth may see
Some work of love begun,
Some deed of kindness done,
Some wanderer sought and won,
Something for Thee.

All that I am and have,
Thy gifts so free,
In joy, in grief, through life,
Dear Lord, for Thee!
And when Thy face I see,
My ransomed soul shall be,
Through all eternity,
Something for Thee.

—*S. D. Phelps*

God's Will For Us

Just to be tender, just to be true;
Just to be glad the whole day through;
Just to be merciful, just to be mild;
Just to be trustful as a child;
Just to be gentle and kind and sweet;
Just to be helpful with willing feet;
Just to be cheery when things go wrong;
Just to drive sadness away with a song,
Whether the hour is dark or bright;
Just to be loyal to God and right;
Just to believe that God knows best;
Just in His promise ever to rest;
Just to let love be our daily key:
This is God's will, for you and me.

—*Anonymous*

In Earthern Vessels

The dear Lord's best interpreters
    Are humble human souls;
The gospel of a life like His
    Is more than books or scrolls.

From scheme and creed the light goes out,
    The saintly fact survives;
The blessed Master none can doubt,
    Revealed in holy lives.

—*John Greenleaf Whittier*

LOVE

The Larger Prayer

At first I prayed for Light:
  Could I but see the way,
How gladly, swiftly would I walk
  To everlasting day!

And next I prayed for Strength:
  That I might tread the road
With firm, unfaltering feet, and win
  The heaven's serene abode.

And then I asked for Faith:
  Could I but trust my God,
I'd live enfolded in His peace,
  Though foes were all abroad.

But now I pray for Love:
  Deep love to God and man,
A living love that will not fail,
  However dark His plan.

And Light and Strength and Faith
  Are opening everywhere.
God waited for me till
  I prayed the larger prayer.
                    —*Ednah D. Cheney*

MERCY

The All-Embracing

There's a wideness in God's mercy,
  Like the wideness of the sea;
There's a kindness in His justice,
  Which is more than liberty.

There is welcome for the sinner,
  And more graces for the good;
There is mercy with the Saviour;
  There is healing in His blood.

For the love of God is broader
  Than the measure of man's mind;
And the heart of the Eternal
  Is most wonderfully kind.

If our love were but more simple,
  We should take Him at His word;
And our lives would be all sunshine
  In the sweetness of our Lord.
                    —*Frederick W. Faber*

MISSIONS

The Clarion-Call

Awake, awake, O Church of God!
  Comes now to thee the call
Of Christ, thy Lord, who bids thee on
  Till every foe shall fall.
What though the hosts of darkness stand,
  Their last fierce battle make?
The Victor, Christ, he summons thee;
  O Church of God, awake!

O Church of God, lose not the day
  What now has come to thee;
A world, awaking from its sleep,
  Is waiting light to see.
On heathen altars fires burn low,
  Forsaken temples are;
Now, now advance, let idols fall,
  And Christ be known afar.

The fathers heard; they followed fast,
   And eager met the foe,
The prison's chain, the dungeon's gloom,
   And drank the cup of woe.
With faith-cleared eye they saw the Lord,
   The meaning of His cross;
For mankind's sake, for Jesus' love,
   All things they counted loss.

The toil and labor of the years,
   Let these not be in vain;
Haste, reap where others sowed in tears,
   And weary served in pain.
Thy sons, thy daughters ready are
   To dare for Jesus' sake;
O golden Hour! what call is thine!
   O Church of God, awake!

—Anonymous

A Cry For Light

There comes a wail of anguish
   Across the ocean wave—
It pleads for help, O Christians,
   Poor dying souls to save.
Those far-off heathen natives,
   Who sit in darkest night,
Now stretch their hands imploring,
   And cry to us for light.

We have the blessed gospel;
   We know its priceless worth;
We read the grand old story
   Of Christ the Saviour's birth.
O haste ye, faithful workers,
   To them the tidings bear—
Glad tidings of salvation,
   That they our light may share.

—Anonymous

Let Me Go Back

Words of a Missionary.

Let me go back! I am homesick
For the land of my love and toil,
Tho' I thrill at the sight of my native hills,
The touch of my native soil.
Thank God for the dear home country,
Unconquered and free and grand!
But the far-off shores of the East, for me,
Are the shores of the Promised Land.

No longer young—I know it—
And battered and worn and gray,
I bear in my body the marks that tell
Of many a toil-filled day.
But 'tis long to the end of a lifetime,
And the hour for the sun to set;
My heart is eager for years to come;
Let me work for the Master yet!

My brain is dazed and wearied
With the New World's stress and strife,
With the race for money and place and power
And the whirl of the nation's life.
Let me go back! Such pleasures
And pains are not for me;
But Oh! for a share in the Harvest Home
Of the fields beyond the sea.

For there are my chosen people,
And that is my place to fill,
To spend the last of my life and strength
In doing my Master's will.
Let me go back! 'Tis nothing
To suffer and do and dare;
For the Lord has faithfully kept His Word,
He is "with me always" there!

—*Mary E. Albright*

Is This the Time To Sound Retreat?

Is this the time, O Church of Christ, to sound
Retreat? To arm with weapons cheap and blunt
The men and women who have borne the brunt
Of truth's fierce strife, and nobly held their ground?
Is this the time to halt, when all around
Horizons lift, new destinies confront,
Stern duties wait our nation, never wont
To play the laggard, when God's will was found?
No! Rather strengthen stakes and lengthen cords,
Enlarge thy plans and gifts, O thou elect,
And to thy kingdom come for such a time!
The earth with all the fulness is the Lord's,
Great things attempt for Him, great things expect!
Whose love imperial is, whose power sublime.

—Oriental Missionary Standard

Daybreak

The morning light is breaking,
    The darkness disappears;
The sons of earth are waking
    To penitential tears;
Each breeze that sweeps the ocean
    Brings tidings from afar
Of nations in commotion,
    Prepared for Zion's war.

See heathen nations bending
    Before the God we love,
And thousand hearts ascending
    In gratitude above;
While sinners now confessing,
    The gospel shall obey,
And seek the Saviour's blessing,
    A nation in a day.

Blest river of salvation,
   Pursue thy onward way;
Flow thou to every nation,
   Nor in thy richness stay;
Stay not till all the lowly
   Triumphant reach their home;
Stay not till all the holy
   Proclaim, "The Lord is come."

—*S. F. Smith*

NEW YEAR'S DAY

Another Year

Another year is dawning!
Dear master, let it be,
In working or in waiting,
Another year with Thee.
Another year in leaning,
Upon Thy loving breast,
Of ever-deepening trustfulness,
Of quiet, happy rest.

Another year of mercies,
Of faithfulness and grace;
Another year of gladness,
In the shining of Thy face.
Another year of progress,
Another year of praise;
Another year of proving
Thy presence "all the days."

Another year of service,
Of witness for Thy love;
Another year of training
For holier works above.

Another year is dawning!
Dear Master, let it be
On earth, or else in heaven,
Another year for Thee!
—*Frances Ridley Havergal*

The New Year

Upon the threshold of the year we stand,
  Holding Thy Hand;
The year holds mysteries and vague surprise
  To meet our eyes;
What will its passing moments bring,
  To weep, or sing?

We fear to take one step without Thy care
  And presence there;
But all is clear to Thine all-seeing gaze,
  Counting the days
From dawn of time, till ages cease to be—
  Eternity!

Upon the threshold of the year we stand,
  Holding Thy Hand;
Thou wilt walk step by step along the way
  With us each day;
So whether joy or woe shall come this year,
  We shall not fear!
—*Homera Homer-Dixon*

The Old Year and the New

Into the Silent Places
  The Old Year goes tonight,
Bearing old pain, old sadness,
  Old care, and old delight,
Mistakes and fears and failures,
  The things that could not last;—
But naught that e'er was truly ours
  Goes with him to the Past.

Out of the Silent Places
The Young Year comes tonight,
Bringing new pain, new sadness,
New care and new delight;
Go forth to meet him bravely,
The New Year all untried,
The things the Old Year left with us—
Faith, Hope, and Love—abide.
—Annie Johnson Flint

The Opening Year

The year is gone, beyond recall,
With all its hopes and fears,
With all its bright and gladdening smiles,
With all its mourners' tears.

Thy thankful people praise thee, Lord,
For countless gifts received;
And pray for grace to keep the faith,
Which saints of old believed.

O Father, let thy watchful eye
Still look on us in love,
That we may praise thee, year by year,
With angel-hosts above.
—From the Latin, Tr. by F. Pott

At the Portal

Standing at the portal
Of the opening year
Words of comfort meet us,
Hushing every fear;
Spoken through the silence
By our Father's voice,
Tender, strong and faithful,
Making us rejoice:

"I, the Lord, am with thee;
  Be thou not afraid!
I will keep and strengthen;
  Be thou not dismayed!
Yea, I will uphold thee
  With my own right hand;
Thou art called and chosen
  In my sight to stand."

For the year before us,
  Oh, what rich supplies!
For the poor and needy
  Living streams shall rise,
For the sad and sinful
  Shall His grace abound;
For the faint and feeble
  Perfect strength be found.

He will never fail us,
  He will not forsake;
His eternal covenant
  He will never break!
Resting on His promise
  What have we to fear?
God is all-sufficient
  For the coming year.
                —*Frances Ridley Havergal*

"Go Forward"

A Motto for the New Year.

With steadfast heart and true
  Go farward on your way;
God give you strength to do
  The duties of each day,
So daily may this thought
  Your heart with courage fill,
"I can, because I ought,
  And, by God's help, I will."

—*A. R. G.*

A Prayer

Through every minute of this day,
  Be with me, Lord!
Through every day of all this week,
  Be with me, Lord!
Through every week of all this year,
  Be with me, Lord!

So shall the days and weeks and years
  Be threaded on a golden cord,
And all draw on with sweet accord
  Unto Thy fullness, Lord;
    That so, when time is past,
    By grace I may at last
    Be with Thee, Lord!

—John Oxenham

(Used by permission of the Author)

Lessons of the Year

For I learn as the years roll onward
  And leave the past behind,
That much I have counted sorrow
  But proves that our God is kind;
That many a flower I longed for
  Had a hidden thorn of pain,
And many a rugged by-path
  Led to fields of golden grain.

The clouds but cover the sunshine,
  They cannot banish the sun,
And the earth looks out the brighter,
  When the wearisome rain is done.
We must stand in the deepest shadow
  To see the clearest light,
And often from wrong's own darkness
  Comes the very strength of right.

The sweetest rest is at evening
    After the wearisome day,
When the heavy burden of labor
    Is borne from our hearts away.
And those who have never known sorrow
    Cannot find the infinite peace
That falls on the troubled spirit,
    When it finds a sweet release.

We must live through the dreary winter
    To value the bright warm spring;
The woods must be cold and silent
    Before the robins sing;
The flowers must be buried in darkness
    Before they can bud and bloom,
And the purest and warmest sunshine
    Comes after the storm and gloom.

So the heart from the hardest trial
    Gains the purest joy of all,
And the lips that have tasted sadness
    The sweetest songs that fall.
Then as joy comes after sorrow,
    And love's the reward of pain,
So after earth is heaven,
    And out of our loss is gain.

—*Anonymous*

God Is Faithful
I. Cor. 10:13.

God will never fail us.
    He will not forsake: :
His eternal covenant
    He will never break.
Resting on His promise,
    What have we to fear?
God is all-sufficient
    For the coming year.

—*F. R. Havergal*

Backward—Forward

I stand upon the threshold of two years,
    And backward look, and forward strain my eyes,
Upon blotted record fall my tears.
    While brushing them aside, a sweet surprise
Breaks like a day-dawn on my upturned face
As I remember all Thy daily grace.

Thou hast been good to me; the burdened past
    Thou hast borne with me, and the future days
Are in Thy hands, I tremble not, but cast
    My care upon Thee, and in prayer and praise,
Prepare to make the coming year the best
Because of nobler work and sweeter rest.

—Anonymous

A New Leaf

He came to my desk with a quivering lip—
    The lesson was done—
"Dear teacher, I want a new leaf," he said;
    "I have spoiled this one."
In place of the leaf so stained and blotted,
I gave him a new one all unspotted,
    And into his sad eyes smiled—
    "Do better now, my child."

I went to the throne with a quivering soul—
    The old year was done—
"Dear Father, hast Thou a new leaf for me?
    I have spoiled this one."
He took the old leaf, stained and blotted,
And gave me a new one all unspotted,
    And into my sad heart smiled—
    "Do better now, my child."

—Anonymous

New Year's Wishes

What shall I wish thee?
Treasures of earth?
Songs in the springtime.
Pleasures and mirth?
Flowers on thy pathway,
Skies ever clear?
Would this insure thee
A Happy New Year?

What shall I wish thee?
What can be found
Bringing thee sunshine
All the year 'round?
Where is the treasure,
Lasting and dear,
That shall ensure thee
A Happy New Year?

Faith that increaseth,
Walking in light;
Hope that aboundeth,
Happy and bright;
Love that is perfect,
Casting out fear;
These shall ensure thee
A Happy New Year.

Peace in the Saviour,
Rest at His feet,
Smile of His countenance
Radiant and sweet,
Joy in His presence!
Christ ever near!
This will ensure thee
A Happy New Year!

—F. R. H.

A New Year Wish

New mercies, new blessings, new light on the way,
New courage, new hope, and new strength for each day;
New wine in the chalice, new altars to raise;
New fruits for thy Master, new garments of praise;
New gifts from his treasures, new smiles from his face;
New streams from the fountain of infinite grace;
New stars for thy crown, and new tokens of love;
New gleams of the glory that waits thee above;
New light of his countenance, full and unpriced—
All this be the joy of thy new year in Christ!

—Frances Ridley Havergal

Old and New

Farewell, Old Year!
With goodness crowned
A hand divine hath set thy bound.

Welcome, New Year,
Which shall bring
Fresh blessings from my God and king!

The old we leave without a tear,
The new we hail without a fear.
Because,
I know that o'er it all
Rules he who notes the sparrow's fall.

—Anonymous

A Prayer for the New Year

I want the New Year's opening days
To fill with love, and prayer, and praise,
Some little things to do for Thee,
For Thou hast done great things for me.

I want some other soul to bring
To Thee, my Saviour and my King.
Thou wilt not, Lord, my prayer deny,
For Thou canst all my wants supply.

In Jesus' name our prayer we raise,
Whose guiding hand has blessed our days.
And may we, Lord, in godly fear
Serve Thee through all this coming year.

—*Anonymous*

A New Year's Wish

"The Lord bless thee, and keep thee: the Lord make his face shine upon thee, and be gracious unto thee: the Lord lift up his countenance upon thee, and give thee peace."—Num. 6:24-26.

God bless thee and keep thee thro' the coming days,
    Give to thy service here His rich increase,
Make His light shine yet brighter on thy ways,
    And crown thee with His own abiding peace!

Cause thee to prove His all-sufficient grace,
    The fulness of His Spirit's power bestow;
Supply the daily strength to run the race,
    And teach thee His blest will to do and know!

Grant thee His presence felt, in woe and weal,
    And evermore His joy—all joys above;
Speak to thine heart more clearly and reveal
    The heights and depths of His unfathomed love!

God bless and keep thee thro' the heat of day,
    Beneath His shield safe-sheltered from all harm,
And when the hours of toil have passed away,
    Grant a bright eventide, and sunset calm!

Then, when all fleeting years of time are gone—
    Their joys and sorrows as a watch of night—
With the fair sunrise of a summer morn
    Shall dawn the glory of eternal light.

—*J. H. S., in "The Christian"*

A Prayer for a Happy New Year

Bless Thou, this year, O Lord!
Make rich its days
With health, and work, and prayer, and praise,
And helpful ministry
To needy folk.
Speak Thy soft word
In cloudy days;
Nor let us think ourselves forgot
When common lot
Of sorrow hems us round.
Let generous impulse shame the niggard dole
That dwarfs the soul.
May no one shirk his share of work
Through selfish thought.
Each day fulfil Thy holy will
In yielded lives;
And still the tumult
Of desires
Debased.
May faith and hope and love,
Inspired from above,
Increase.
Bless Thou, this year, O Lord!

—*Andrew S. C. Clarke*

A New Year Wish

What shall I wish thee this New Year?
Health, wealth, prosperity, good cheer,
All sunshine—not a cloud or tear?
   Nay! only this:
That God may lead thee His own way,
That He may choose thy path each day,
That thou mayest feel Him near alway,
   For this is bliss!

—*Anonymous*

"I Am With Thee"

Exo. 33:15-19, Mt. 28:20, Isa. 41:10.

We're crossing the bar of another year—
    How swiftly they come and go!
We shall meet them all without any fear—
    Our Father has taught us so.

As Moses once asked to be shown God's way,
    We earnestly oft have prayed!
Then the answer came and we heard Him say:
    "I am with thee—be not afraid!"

So we face the future with fearless heart,
    If easy the work or rough,
For when He goes with us, He takes our part,
    He keeps us—that is enough.

O heart that is troubled with burdens today,
    Look up to your God on high,
He'll carry the brunt of the battle long,
    In danger be ever nigh!
                                    —*Rev. Ernest Bourner Allen*

Confidence

I do not know, I cannot see,
What God's kind hand prepares for me,
Nor can my glance pierce through the haze,
Which covers all my future ways;
But yet I know that o'er it all
Rules He who notes the sparrow's fall.

Farewell, Old Year, with goodness crowned,
A hand divine hath set my bound,
Welcome the New Year, which shall bring
Fresh blessings from my God and King.
The Old we leave without a tear,
The New we hail without a fear.
                                    —*Anonymous*

A New Year's Promise

Another year I enter,
  Its history unknown;
Oh, how my feet would tremble
  To tread its paths alone!
But I have heard a whisper;
  I know I shall be blest:
"My presence shall go with thee
  And I will give thee rest."

What will the New Year bring me?
  I may not, must not know;
Will it be love and rapture,
  Or loneliness and woe?
Hush! hush! I hear His whisper;
  I surely shall be blest:
"My presence shall go with thee
  And I will give thee rest."

—Anonymous

All Thro' the Year

The world's a weary place,
For him who tries to face
  His tasks alone.
But he who looks above,
Will see the God of love
Is always swift to move
  Among His own.

And so I wish for thee
The vision clear to see,
  A presence near;
That every hour of night
And all the days of light,
May with God's love shine bright
  All thro' the year.

—Anonymous

Facing the New Year

Fear, facing the New Year
Saith, What shall it bring?
    And is dumb,
Dreading the hidden ways.
Faith, looking upward, saith
Good is in everything.
    Let it come.
God ordereth the days.
This is our New Year's bliss,
He is mine, and I am His.
All the ways, all the days,
    Lead us home.
Let us pray: Let us praise.

—*Mark Guy Pearse*

New Time

Time is a treasure;
    How shall we use it?
We can make useful,
    Or can abuse it!
Only the Giver
    Can make our hearts wise,
Teaching us daily
    The New Time to prize.

Time is a treasure,
    So view it, my soul!
Keep all its spending
    'Neath watchful control;
Employ each moment
    In God's holy fear,
And He will ensure thee
    A Happy New Year.

—*Anonymous*

OBEDIENCE

Get Somebody Else

The Lord had a job for me,
　But I had so much to do,
I said, "You get somebody else,
　Or wait till I get through."
I don't know how the Lord came out,
　But He seemed to get along,
But I felt kind o' sneakin' like—
　Knowed I'd done God wrong.

One day I needed the Lord—
　Needed Him right away;
But He never answered me at all,
　And I could hear Him say,
Down in my accusin' heart:
　"Nigger, I'se got too much to do;
You get somebody else,
　Or wait till I get through."

Now, when the Lord He have a job for me,
　I never tries to shirk;
I drops what I have on hand,
　And does the good Lord's work.
And my affairs can run along,
　Or wait till I get through;
Nobody else can do the work
　That God marked out for you.
　　　　　　—Paul Lawrence Dunbar

Obedience

I said, "Let me walk in the fields";
　He said, "Nay, walk in the town";
I said, "There are no flowers there";
　He said, "No flowers, but a crown."

I said, "But the sky is black,
   There is nothing but noise and din."
But He wept as He sent me back;
   "There is more," He said, "there is sin."

I said, "But the air is thick,
   And fogs are veiling the sun."
He answered, "Yet hearts are sick,
   And souls in the dark undone."

I said, "I shall miss the light,
   And friends will miss me, they say."
He answered me, "Choose to-night
   If I am to miss you, or they."

I pleaded for time to be given;
   He said, "Is it hard to decide?
It will not seem hard in heaven
   To have followed the steps of your guide."

I cast one look at the field,
   Then set my face to the town;
He said, "My child, do you yield?
   Will you leave the flowers for the crown?"

Then into His hand went mine,
   And into my heart came He,
And I walk in a light divine
   The path I had feared to see!"
                —George MacDonald

PEACE

Peace, Perfect Peace

"Thou wilt keep him in perfect peace whose mind is stayed on thee."—Isaiah 26:3.

Peace, perfect peace, in this dark world of sin:
   The Blood of Jesus whispers "Peace" within.
Peace, perfect peace, by thronging duties pressed:
   To do the Will of Jesus—this is rest.

Peace, perfect peace, with sorrows surging round:
On Jesus' bosom naught but calm is found.
Peace, perfect peace, our future all unknown:
Jesus we know—and He is on the Throne.

Peace, perfect peace, Death shadowing us and ours:
Jesus has vanquished Death and all its powers.
It is enough!   Earth's struggles soon shall cease.
And Jesus call us to Heaven's perfect peace.

—*Edward H. Bickersteth*

PENTECOST

A Prayer for Pentecost

A rushing wind the Spirit came!
Purge us from all that would defame,
O Cleansing One.

Our sins lost in Thy holiness,
Let worthy lives our faith confess,
O Sinless Son.

The gift of tongues the Spirit brought!
May our dull tongues by Thee be taught,
Master of Love.

May words and deeds tell every land
The word we preach at Love's command,
Father above.

The Spirit came in tongues of fire!
Now our cold hearts with flame inspire,
Spirit Divine.

Give us a holy zeal for Thee
To labor for eternity,
Our wills all Thine.

—*Catherine Bernard Brown*

A Call To Pentecost

Full nineteen centuries have passed since then,
How changed, for us the world since that blest hour;
The church was born through Pentecostal power,
When the Holy Spirit filled the hearts of men.
Disciples, once so weak, waxed bold and strong,
Christ's witnesses, with one accord, they prayed;
They shared their joy, all conquering, unafraid;
Christ's name was glorified in prayer and song.

So may we, Lord, bear witness, as of old,
Filled with His Spirit, let "dumb tongues unloose,"
Let brotherhood drive out all greed and hate;
The "fires of God" can warm and melt and mould,
The "gales of God" can bear us on in love,
Dynamic guide of all, we pray, we wait.

—*Inez M. Tyler*

POVERTY

"Borrowed"

They borrowed a bed to lay His head,
When Christ the Lord came down,
They borrowed an ass in the mountain pass
For Him to ride to town.
  But the crown that He wore
  And the cross that He bore
    Were His own.

He borrowed the bread when the crowd He fed
On the grassy mountain side;
He borrowed the dish of broken fish
With which He satisfied.
  But the crown that He wore
  And the cross that He bore
    Were His own.

He borrowed the ship in which to sit
To teach the multitude,
He borrowed the nest in which to rest,
He had never a home as rude,
  But the crown that He wore
  And the cross that He bore
    Were His own.

He borrowed a room on the way to the tomb,
The passover lamb to eat.
They borrowed a cave, for Him a grave,
They borrowed a winding sheet.
  But the crown that He wore
  And the cross that He bore
    Were His own.

The thorns on His head were worn in my stead,
For me the Saviour died;
For guilt of my sin the nails drove in
When Him they crucified.
  Though the crown that He wore
  And the cross that He bore
    Were His own,
They rightly were mine—instead.

—Anonymous

Poor for Our Sakes

The earth, with all its fullness, is the Lord's:
  He made it, and 'tis His alone for aye;
Yet in a borrowed bed in Bethlehem
  They laid Him, when He came to earth one day.

The sea is His, and all its mighty waves
  He holds within the hollow of His hand;
Yet 'tis a borrowed boat He needs must use
  To put out from that thronged Gennesaret strand.

The cattle o'er a thousand hills are His,
  The fruitage too that countless valleys yield;
Yet He must borrow bread and fish to feed
  The hungry people in Bethsaida's field.

And all the silver and the gold are His,
    With all earth holds of treasures rich and vast;
Yet in a borrowed room He spread a feast,
    And in a borrowed tomb was laid at last.

Yea, for our sake, He laid His wealth aside;
    Yet from His poverty such blessing streams,
That we, the very poorest of the poor,
    Are rich beyond all counting and all dreams.
                                    —*Mary Brainerd Smith*

PRAYER

Prevailing Prayer

Lord, what a change within us one short hour
Spent in Thy presence would prevail to make!
What heavy burdens from our bosoms take,
What parched grounds revive as with a shower;
We kneel, and all around us seems to lower;
We rise, and all, the distant and the near
Stands forth a sunny outline brave and clear.
We kneel, how weak! we arise, how full of power!
Why, therefore, should we do ourselves this wrong,
Or others, that we are not always strong;
That we are ever overborne with care;
That we should ever weak or heartless be,
Anxious or troubled, when with us is prayer,
And joy and strength and courage are with Thee?
                                    —*Archbishop Trench*

His Presence Came Like Sunrise

I met God in the morning,
    When my day was at its best,
And His presence came like sunrise,
    Like a glory in my breast.

All day long the presence lingered;
   All day long He stayed with me;
And we sailed in perfect calmness
   O'er a very troubled sea.

Other ships were blown and battered,
   Other ships were sore distressed,
But the winds that seemed to drive them
   Brought to us a peace and rest.

Then I thought of other mornings,
   With a keen remorse of mind,
When I too had loosed the moorings
   With the presence left behind.

So I think I know the secret
   Learned from many a troubled way:
You must seek Him in the morning
   If you want Him through the day.
                    —*Ralph S. Cushman*

The Unfailing Friend

What a friend we have in Jesus,
   All our sins and griefs to bear;
What a privilege to carry
   Everything to God in prayer,
Oh, what peace we often forfeit,
   Oh, what needless pain we bear—
All because we do not carry
   Everything to God in prayer.

Have we trials and temptations?
   Is there trouble anywhere?
We should never be discouraged;
   Take it to the Lord in prayer.
Can we find a Friend so faithful,
   Who will all our sorrows share?
Jesus knows our every weakness,
   Take it to the Lord in prayer.

Are we weak and heavy-laden,
  Cumbered with a load of care?
Precious Saviour, still our Refuge,—
  Take it to the Lord in prayer.
Do thy friends despise, forsake thee?
  Take it to the Lord in prayer;
In His arms He'll take and shield thee,
  Thou wilt find a solace there.

                   —*Joseph Scriven*

Sometime—Somewhere

Unanswered yet? the prayer your lips have pleaded
In agony of heart these many years?
Does faith begin to fail, is hope declining,
And think you all in vain those falling tears?
Say not the Father hath not heard your prayer,
You shall have your desire sometime, somewhere.

Unanswered yet? Faith cannot be unanswered,
Her feet are firmly planted on the Rock;
Amid the wildest storms she stands undaunted,
Nor quails before the loudest thunder shock,
She knows Omnipotence has heard her prayer,
And cries, "It shall be done, sometime, somewhere!"

               —*Mrs. Ophelia G. Browning*

Prayer

More things are wrought by Prayer
Than this world dreams of. Wherefore, let thy voice
Rise like a fountain for me night and day.
For what are men better than sheep or goats
That nourish a blind life within the brain,
If, knowing God, they lift not hands of prayer
Both for themselves and those who call them friend?
For so the whole round earth is every way
Bound by gold chains about the feet of God.

               —*Alfred, Lord Tennyson*

What Is Prayer?

Prayer is the soul's sincere desire,
   Utter'd or unexpress'd;
The motion of a hidden fire
   That trembles in the breast.

Prayer is the burthen of a sigh,
   The falling of a tear,
The upward glancing of the eye,
   When none but God is near.

Prayer is the simplest form of speech
   That infant lips can try;
Prayer the sublimest strains that reach
   The Majesty on high.

Prayer is the contrite sinner's voice
   Returning from his ways,
While angels in their songs rejoice,
   And cry, Behold, he prays!

Prayer is the Christian's vital breath,
   The Christian's native air;
His watchword at the gates of death;
   He enters heaven with prayer.

The saints in prayer appear as one
   In word, and deed, and mind;
While with the Father and the Son
   Sweet fellowship they find.

Nor prayer is made by man alone:
   The Holy Spirit pleads;
And Jesus, on the eternal Throne,
   For mourners intercedes.

O Thou, by whom we come to God!
   The Life, the Truth, the Way!
The path of prayer Thyself hast trod:
   Lord! teach us how to pray!

                        —James Montgomery

Sweet Hour of Prayer

Sweet hour of prayer! sweet hour of prayer!
That calls me from a world of care,
And bids me at my Father's throne
Make all my wants and wishes known.
In seasons of distress and grief
My soul has often found relief,
||:And oft escaped the tempter's snare
By thy return, sweet hour of prayer!

Sweet hour of prayer! sweet hour of prayer!
Thy wings shall my petition bear
To Him whose truth and faithfulness
Engage the waiting soul to bless.
And since He bids me seek His face,
Believe His word, and trust His grace,
||: I'll cast on Him my every care,
And wait for thee, sweet hour of prayer!

Sweet hour of prayer! sweet hour of prayer!
May I thy consolation share,
Till, from Mount Pisgah's lofty height,
I view my home and take my flight;
This robe of flesh I'll drop, and rise
To seize the everlasting prize;
||:And shout, while passing through the air,
Farewell, farewell, sweet hour of prayer!
—*W. W. Walford*

To Begin the Day

A moment in the morning, ere the cares of day begin,
Ere the heart's wide door is open for the world to enter in;
Ah, then alone with Jesus, in the silence of the morn,
In heavenly, sweet communion let your duty day be born.
In the quietude that blesses with a prelude of repose,
Let your soul be soothed and softened, as the dew revives
the rose.

A moment in the morning, take your Bible in your hand,
And catch a glimpse of glory from the peaceful promised
    land;
It will linger still before you when you seek the busy mart,
And, like flowers of hope, will blossom into beauty in your
    heart;
The precious words, like jewels, will glisten all the day,
With a rare, effulgent glory that will brighten all the way.

A moment in the morning—a moment, if no more—
Is better than an hour when the trying day is o'er.
'Tis the gentle dew from heaven, the manna for the day;
If you fail to gather early—alas! it melts away.
So, in the blush of morning take the offered hand of love,
And walk in heaven's pathway and the peacefulness thereof.

—Anonymous

Pray!

"Men ought always to pray."—Luke 18:1.

Pray in the early morning
    For grace throughout the day;
We know not what temptations
    And trials may cross our way.

Pray in the gladsome noontide,
    When the day is at its best;
Pray when the night o'ertakes thee
    To Him who giveth rest.

Pray in the silent midnight,
    If wakeful hours be thine;
Pray for a heart submissive,
    That never will repine.

Pray in the hour of sorrow,
    Pray in the hour of grief;
In coming to the Father,
    Thy soul shall find relief.

Pray when the sun shines brightest,
  Thy path with roses strewn;
Pray that thy heart be ever
  With the Saviour's kept in tune.

Pray when the dark day cometh,
  And clouds hang overhead;
In the secret of His presence
  Thy soul hath naught to dread.

Pray for the Father's guidance
  In all thy work and ways,
So shall thy days be fruitful,
  Thy life be full of praise.

Living in touch with Jesus,
  Keeping our own hearts right,
Others will be attracted
  From darkness into light.
              —*Mrs. Major Arnold*

The Sentinel

The morning is the gate of day,
  But ere you enter there
See that you set to guard it well
  The sentinel of prayer.
So shall God's grace your steps attend,
  But nothing else pass through
Save what can give the countersign;
  The Father's will for you.

When you have reached the end of day
  Where night and sleep await,
Set there the sentinel again
  To bar the evening's gate.
So shall no fear disturb your rest,
  No danger and no care.
For only peace and pardon pass
  The watchful guard of prayer.
              —*The British Weekly*

My Prayer

Not in the silence only,
  Nor in the solitude,
Let my thoughts rise to Thee in praise,
  My God, so great, so good.

But mid the din and noise
  Of city conflict rude;
In crowded street where daily pours
  The hurrying multitude.

Not on the Sabbath only,
  In the dear house of prayer,
Where earthly din cannot intrude,
  And only God is there.

But all week long, in spite
  Of care and vanity;
That thus, even in the crowd, I may
  Be still alone with Thee.

—*Horatius Bonar*

De Profundis

Out of the depths have I cried unto Thee, O Lord.
Lord, hear my voice; let Thine ears be attentive to the
  voice of my supplications.
If Thou, O Lord, shouldst mark iniquities, who shall stand?
But there is forgiveness with Thee, that Thou mayest be
  feared.
I wait for the Lord, my soul doth wait, and in His word do
  I hope.
My soul waiteth for the Lord more than they that watch
  for the morning; I say, more than they that watch for
  the morning.
Let Israel hope in the Lord; for with the Lord there is
  mercy, and with Him is plenteous redemption.
And He shall redeem Israel from all his iniquities.

—*Psalm 130 (King James Ver.)*

The Quiet Hour

Alone with God for one sweet, solemn hour,
The quiet charm enfolds in peace and power,
And love steals o'er the heart a radiant shower,
Ennobling and enriching by its dower!

Alone with God upon the sunlit height,
When glorious morn dispels the gloom of night,
When the evil fades and all is good and right,
When hearts are strengthened for the coming fight!

Alone with God, oh, blessed hour of prayer,
When men with the dear Maker all may share,
And on Him lay the burden of life's care,
Which grows too great for human hearts to bear.

Alone with God, oh, priceless gift so rare,
When comes the heartening to do and dare,
Emboldened by the spirit of true prayer,
That speaks the words of life so pure and fair!
                    —*Louise Hollingsworth Bowman*

Keep on Praying

Keep on praying—God's love and power
In darkest hour of deep despair
    Responds to prayer.

Keep on praying—be not afraid
To seek His aid who knows indeed
    Thine every need.

Keep on praying—in thy distress
He waits to bless; To Him reveal
    All thou dost feel.

Keep on praying—He'll answer thee;
And it may be His love will bring
    Some better thing.

Keep on praying—e'en though in death
With parting breath; He will forgive
    And bid thee live.

Keep on praying—His heart divine
Will enter thine, and lead the way
    To blissful day.

                        —*Roger H. Lyon*

An Evening Prayer

If aught I may have said or done
Hath from the wrong a wanderer won,
    I thank thee, Lord.

If aught I may have said today,
Hath caused one soul to go astray,
    Forgive me, Lord.

So help me live for thee, each day
That some lone traveler on life's way
    May know thee, Lord.

And when at last I see thy face,
And come unto thee, saved by grace,
    Receive me, Lord.

                        —*Laura E. Kendall*

Submission and Rest

The camel, at the close of day,
    Kneels down upon the sandy plain
To have his burden lifted off,
    And rest to gain.

My soul, thou, too, shouldst to thy knees
    When daylight draweth to a close,
And let thy Master lift the load
    And grant repose.

Else how couldst thou to-morrow meet,
  With all to-morrow's work to do,
If thou thy burden all the night
  Dost carry through?

The camel kneels at break of day
  To have his guide replace the load,
Then rises up anew to take
  The desert road.

So thou shouldst kneel at morning's dawn,
  That God may give thee daily care,
Assured that He no load too great
  Will make thee bear.

—Anonymous

After the Rain

The withering grass knows not its needs;
  The falling rain knows not its worth;
But God the silent suffering heeds,
  And bids his showers refresh the earth.

My drooping heart oft may not know
  What things to pray for as I ought;
But God will needed good bestow,
  Beyond what I have asked or thought.

—Edward A. Collier

Communion

Don't neglect the quiet hour,
  For the soul that truly seeks
Knows the thrill of holy power—
  Hears the Father when He speaks.

In prayer, by faith, His voice is heard;
  Our inmost soul is strongly stirred;
All loosened cords are brought in tune,
  And we with God Himself commune.

—J. L. Spicer

Ask, and Ye Shall Receive

O praying one, who long has prayed,
  And yet no answer heard,
Have ye been sometimes half afraid
  God might not keep His word?
Seems prayer to fall on deafened ears?
  Does Heaven seem blind and dumb?
Is hope deferred?   Believe—believe—
  The answer time will come!

"Ask what ye will"—His word is true,
  His power is all divine;
Ye cannot test His love too far;
  His utmost shall be thine.
God does not mock believing prayer;
  Ye shall not go unfed!
He gives no serpent for a fish,
  Nor gives He stones for bread.

Thy inmost longings may be told;
  The hopes that turned to shame,
The empty life, the thwarted plans;
  The good that never came.
Say not, "Thy promise is not mine,
  God did not hear me pray;
I prayed—I trusted fully—but
  The grave hath barred the way."

God heard thee—He hath not forgot,
  Faith shall at length prevail!
Yea—know it!   Not one smallest jot
  Of all His word can fail.
For if ye truly have believed,
  Not vain hath been thy prayer!
As God is true, thy hope shall come—
  Sometime, someway, somewhere.

—*Mrs. Havens*

Table Graces, or Prayers

FOR ADULTS

MORNING MEAL

O come, our Lord and Saviour,
  And be our guest today,
That each may have a blessing
  From Thee to take away. Amen.

NOON MEAL

Be present at our table, Lord;
Be here, as everywhere, adored;
These bounties bless and grant that we
May feast in Paradise with Thee.

EVENING MEAL

We thank Thee, Lord, for this our food,
But thank Thee more for Jesus' blood;
May manna to our souls be given,
The bread of life sent down from Heaven.

Great God, Thou giver of all good,
Accept our praise and bless our food.
Grace, health, and strength to us afford,
Through Jesus Christ, our risen Lord. Amen.

FOR CHILDREN

We thank Thee for the morning light,
For rest and shelter of the night,
For health and food, for love and friends,
For everything Thy goodness sends. Amen.

God is great and God is good,
We will thank Him for this food;
By His hand we all are fed,
Give us, Lord, our daily bread. Amen.

God bless this food, and bless us all,
And keep us safe, whate'er befall.
For Jesus' sake. Amen.

Heavenly Father, bless this food
To Thy glory and our good. Amen.

Prayer

I know not by what methods rare,
But this I know, God answers prayer.
I know that He has given His Word,
Which tells me prayer is always heard,
And will be answered, soon or late.
And so I pray and calmly wait.
I know not if the blessing sought
Will come in just the way I thought;
But leave my prayers with him alone,
Whose will is wiser than my own,
Assured that He will grant my quest,
Or send some answer far more blest.
—*Eliza M. Hickok*

A Prayer-Poem

God, who touchest earth with beauty,
    Make me lovely too.
With Thy spirit recreate me.
    Make my life anew.

Like Thy springs of running water
    Make me crystal pure.
Like Thy rocks of towering grandeur
    Make me strong and sure.

Like Thy dancing waves in sunlight
    Make me glad and free.
Like the straightness of the pine-tree
    Help me upright be.

Like the arching of Thy heavens,
Raise my thoughts above.
Turn my dreams to noble actions,
Ministries of love.

God, who touchest earth with beauty,
Make me lovely too,
Keep me ever, by Thy Spirit,
Pure and strong and true.

—*Mary S. Adgar*

Children's Prayers

In the bedtime hour there should be prayers at the mother's knee and none are better than "Our Father Who Art in Heaven" and the old and dear:

Now I lay me down to sleep,
I pray the Lord my soul to keep;
If I should die before I wake,
I pray the Lord my soul to take.

The corresponding morning prayer is:

Now I wake and see the light,
'Tis God who kept me through the night.
To Him I lift my voice and pray
That He will keep me through the day.

Both these prayers are fitly concluded with "For Jesus' Sake. Amen."

—*Eugene Henry Pullen*

Jesus Tender Shepherd

One of the best-loved bedtime hymns for children.

Jesus, tender Shepherd, hear me,
Bless Thy little lamb to-night;
Through the darkness be Thou near me,
Keep me safe till morning light.

Through this day Thy hand hath led us,
  And I thank Thee for Thy care;
Thou hast warmed me, clothed and fed me,
  Listen to my evening prayer.

Let my sins be all forgiven,
  Bless the friends I love so well;
Take me when I die to heaven,
  Happy there with Thee to dwell.

—*Mary L. Duncan*

A Child's Prayer

Father, lead me, day by day,
Ever in Thine own sweet way;
Teach me to be pure and true,
Show me what I ought to do.

When I'm tempted to do wrong,
Make me stedfast, wise and strong;
And when all alone I stand,
Shield me with Thy mighty hand.

When my heart is full of glee,
Help me to remember Thee—
Happy most of all to know
That my Father loves me so.

May I do the good I know,
Be Thy loving child below.
Then at last go home to Thee,
Evermore Thy child to be.

—*Anonymous*

The Housewife

Jesus, teach me how to be
Proud of my simplicity.

Sweep the floors, wash the clothes,
Gather for each vase a rose.

Iron and mend a tiny frock,
Keeping one eye on the clock.

Always having time kept free
For childish questions asked of me.

Grant me wisdom Mary had
When she taught her little Lad.

—*Catherine Cate Coblentz*

My Father's Voice In Prayer

In the silence that falls on my spirit
  When the clamor of life loudest seems,
Comes a voice that floats in tremulous notes
  Far over my sea of dreams.
I remember the family altar,
  And my father kneeling there:
And the old tones thrill with the memory still,
  Of my father's voice in prayer.

I can see the glance of approval
  As my part in the reading I took;
I remember the grace of my mother's face,
  And the tenderness of her look;
And I know that a gracious memory
  Cast its light on that face so fair,
As her cheek, flushed faint—O mother, my saint!—
  At my father's voice in prayer.

'Neath the stress of that marvelous pleading
  All childish dissensions died;
Each rebellious will sank conquered and still
  In a passion of love and pride.
Ah, the years have held dear voices,
  And melodies tender and rare,
But tenderest seems the voice of my dreams—
  My father's voice in prayer.

—*May Hastings Nottage*

"The Divine Office of the Kitchen"

Under this heading the Author gives answer to many who complain about having to do the plainer work of this world. She had a friend who complained that domestic drudgery was spoiling her hands for violin playing and sent her these verses.

"God walks among the pots and pipkins."—St. Teresa.

Lord of the pots and pipkins, since I have not time to be
A saint by doing things and vigiling with Thee,
By watching the twilight dawn and storming Heaven's
   gates,
Make me a saint by getting meals and washing up the
   plates.
Lord of the pots and pipkins, please, I offer Thee for souls,
The tiresomeness of tea leaves and the sticky porridge
   bowls!
Remind me of the things I need, not just to save the stairs,
But so that I may perfectly lay tables into prayers.

Accept my roughened hands because I made them so for
   Thee;
Pretend my dish moy is a bow which heavenly harmony
Makes on a fiddle frying pan; it is so hard to clean,
And, oh, so horrid!   Hear, dear Lord, the music that I
   mean.
Although I must have Martha's hands, I have a Mary
   mind.
And when I black the boots, I try Thy sandals, Lord, to
   find;
I think of how they trod our earth, what time I scrub the
   floor—
Accept this meditation when I haven't time for more.

Vespers and compline come to pass by washing supper
   things,
And, mostly, I am very tired, and all the heart that sings
About the morning's work is gone, before me, into bed.
Lend me, dear Lord, Thy tireless heart, to work in me
   instead.

My matins are said overnight to praise and bless Thy name
Beforehand for tomorrow's work, which will be just the
  same;
So that it seems I go to bed still in my working dress.
Lord, make Thy Cinderella soon a heavenly Princess.

Warm all the kitchen with Thy love and light it with Thy
  peace.
Forgive the worrying and make the grumbling words to
  cease.
Lord, who laid breakfast on the shore, forgive the world
  which saith,
"Can any good thing come to God out of poor Nazareth?"
—Cecily Hallack

I Thank Thee, Lord

I thank Thee, Lord, for mine unanswered prayers,
  Unanswered save Thy quiet, kindly "Nay,"
Yet it seemed hard among my heavy cares
  That bitter day.

I wanted joy; but Thou didst know for me
  That sorrow was the gift I needed most,
And in its mystic depth I learned to see
  The Holy Ghost.

I wanted health; but Thou didst bid me sound
  The secret treasuries of pain,
And in the moans and groans my heart oft found
  Thy Christ again.

I wanted wealth: 'twas not the better part,
  There is a wealth with poverty oft given,
And thou didst teach me of the gold of heart,
  Best gift of heaven.

I thank Thee, Lord, for these unanswered prayers,
  And for Thy word, the quiet, kindly "Nay."
'Twas Thy withholding lightened all my cares
  That blessed day.
—Anonymous

For Every Day

SUNDAY.

Lord, speak to me, that I may speak
In living echoes of Thy tone;
As Thou hast sought, so let me seek
Thy erring children lost and lone.

MONDAY.

O lead me, Lord, that I may lead
The wandering and the wavering feet;
O feed me, Lord, that I may feed
Thy hungering ones with manna sweet.

TUESDAY.

O strengthen me, that while I stand
Firm on the Rock, and strong in Thee,
I may stretch out a loving hand
To wrestlers with the troubled sea.

WEDNESDAY.

O teach me, Lord, that I may teach
The precious things Thou dost impart;
And wing my words that they may reach
The hidden depths of many a heart.

THURSDAY.

O give Thine own sweet rest to me,
That I may speak with soothing power
A word in season, as from Thee,
To weary ones in needful hour.

FRIDAY.

O fill me with Thy fulness, Lord,
Until my very heart o'erflow
In kindling thought and glowing word,
Thy love to tell, Thy praise to show.

SATURDAY,

O use me, Lord, use even me,
  Just as Thou wilt, and when, and where,
Until Thy blessed face I see—
  Thy rest, Thy joy, Thy glory share!
                —*Frances Ridley Havergal*

The Two Prayers

Last night my boy confessed to me
Some childish wrong;
And kneeling at my knee
He prayed with tears:
"Dear God, make me a man,
Like Daddy—wise and strong;
I know You can."

Then while he slept
I knelt beside his bed,
Confessed my sins,
And prayed with love-bowed head,
"Oh God, make me a child
Like my child here—
Pure, guileless,
Trusting Thee with faith sincere."
                —*Andrew Gillies*
(Used by permission of the Author)

When I Had Need of Him

I had forgotten how to pray,
  I had forgotten God,
For it had been an easy way
  That I serenely trod.
Untroubled, I had ceased to care
  How others failed or fell,
But in my moment of despair
  Oh, I remembered well!

The clouds grew dark above my head,
   My ceaseless laughter died;
I found myself oppressed by dread,
   And cast away my pride.
The friends to whom I once had turned
   Could serve my needs no more;
There was a lesson I had learned—
   I, who had laughed before.

I looked upon Fear's ugly shape,
   I felt the clutch of Woe;
There seemed no promise of escape,
   Hell opened wide below!
Behind my closet door I crept,
   Where no one might perceive,
And there I knelt and prayed and wept,
   Still eager to believe.

Untroubled, I had turned from prayer
   To seek the things that please,
But in my moment of despair
   I fell upon my knees.
Cheered by the light that had so long
   Seemed far away and dim,
My faith in God was sure and strong
   When I had need of Him.

—*S. E. Kiser*

(Used by permission of the Author)

My Prayer

Lord Jesus, make Thyself to me
A living, bright reality;
More present to faith's vision keen
Than any outward object seen;
More dear, more intimately nigh
Then e'en the sweetest earthly tie."

—*Anonymous*

My Prayer

My life must touch a million lives in some way ere I go
From this dear world of struggle to the land I do not know.
So this wish I always wish, the prayer I ever pray:
Let my life help the other lives it touches by the way!

—Anonymous

Because We Do Not See

The weary one had rest, the sad had joy that day,
    And wondered how?
A ploughman singing at his work had prayed,
    "Lord, help them now."
Away in foreign lands they wondered how
    Their feeble words had power?
At home the Christians, two or three had met
    To pray an hour.
Yes, we are always wondering, wondering how,
    Because we do not see
Some one unknown perhaps, and far away,
    On bended knee.

—Anonymous

PROMISES OF GOD

God's Promises

As the deep blue of heaven brightens into stars,
So God's great love shines forth in promises.
Which, falling softly through our prison bars,
Daze not our eyes, but with their sweet light bless.
Ladders of light, God sets against the skies,
Upon whose golden rungs we step by step arise.

—Anonymous

REST

The Call to the Strong

Not to the weak alone
Soundeth the call of Love,
   "Come unto me and rest";
But to the spirits strong and great,
Who do the work and bear the weight,
Toiling from early morn till late,
   With vigor and grace and zest.

These are the lives that labor,
These are the heavy laden,
   Theirs is the blessed word.
Not for themselves the strain and care
It is their neighbor's grief they share,
It is their brother's load they bear,
   Even as did their Lord.

Patient they are, and brave,
Steadily marching on,
   Ready for every test.
Only the Lord who trod that way
Knows of the strain from day to day,
Knows how they long to hear him say,
   "Come unto me and rest."

And it is sweet to know
How to each broken heart
   Cometh the summons blest:
"Ye who have toiled without avail,
Ye who were tempted but to fail,
Ye who are sad and poor and frail,
   'Come unto me and rest.'"

Yet there is something more,
Better and worthier far,
   Richest reward and best:

"Ye who are strong and true and brave,
Putting aside the ease ye crave,
Comrades of him who died to save,
'Come unto me and rest.' "
—*William Pierson Merrill*
(Used by permission of the Author)

SALVATION THROUGH CHRIST

Rock of Ages

Rock of Ages, cleft for me,
Let me hide myself in Thee;
Let the water and the blood,
From Thy riven side which flowed,
Be of sin the double cure,
Save me from its guilt and power.

Not the labor of my hands
Can fulfil Thy law's demands;
Could my zeal no respite know,
Could my tears forever flow,
All for sin could not atone;
Thou must save, and Thou alone.

Nothing in my hand I bring,
Simply to Thy cross I cling;
Naked, come to Thee for dress,
Helpless, look to Thee for grace;
Foul, I to the fountain fly,
Wash me, Saviour, or I die.

While I draw this fleeting breath,
While mine eyes shall close in death,
When I soar to worlds unknown,
See Thee on Thy judgment throne,
Rock of Ages, cleft for me,
Let me hide myself in Thee.
—*Augustus Montague Toplady*

I Know a Name!

I know a soul that is steeped in sin,
  That no man's art can cure;
But I know a Name, a precious Name,
  That can make that soul all pure.

I know a life that is lost to God,
  Bound down by things of earth;
But I know a Name, a precious Name,
  That can bring that soul new birth.

I know of lands that are sunk in shame,
  Of hearts that faint and tire;
But I know a Name, a precious Name,
  That can set those lands on fire.

I know a Name, a precious Name,
  Its sound is a brand, its letters flame,
I know a Name, a precious Name,
  That will set those lands on fire.

—*Anonymous*

SATISFACTION

Satisfied

I tried to live by bread alone—
  The bread of earthly store;
But in my grasp it turned to stone:
  I hungered more and more.
I came to Christ, the Living Bread,
  In hungry need I cried;
I feasted at His table spread,
  And I was satisfied.

I tried to walk by human sight,
  With wisdom of my own:
The way grew dark with shades of night;
  I wandered far and lone.
I heard a Voice: "I am the Way;"
  And from the darkness dim
He led me into perfect day;
  And now I walk with Him.

The blessed Saviour is my Guide,
  With Him I can not stray;
My every need is well supplied,
  Through every passing day.
Our sweet companionship, begun,
  Shall last for evermore;
Through life, through death, beyond the sun,
  On heaven's eternal shore.

—Edgar Cooper Mason
(Used by permission of the Author)

SECURITY

The Ninetieth Psalm

O God, our help in ages past,
  Our hope for years to come,
Our shelter from the stormy blast,
  And our eternal home!

Under the shadow of thy throne
  Still may we dwell secure;
Sufficient is thine arm alone,
  And our defense is sure.

Before the hills in order stood,
  Or earth received her frame,
From everlasting Thou art God,
  To endless years the same.

A thousand ages in thy sight,
  Are like an evening gone;
Short as the watch that ends the night,
  Before the rising sun.

The busy tribes of flesh and blood,
  With all their cares and fears,
Are carried downward by the flood,
  And lost in following years.

Time, like an ever-rolling stream,
  Bears all its sons away;
They fly, forgotten, as a dream
  Dies at the opening day.

O God, our help in ages past,
  Our hope for years to come;
Be Thou our guide while life shall last,
  And our eternal home!
                —*Isaac Watts' Lyrical Version*

"In Him"

"We know that we dwell in Him."—I. John 4:13.

"We dwell in Him,"—oh, everlasting Home,
  Imperishable House not made with hands!
When all the world has melted as a dream,
  Eternal in the heav'ns this dwelling stands.
                —*Annie Johnson Flint*
        (Used by permission of the Author)

SOUL WINNING

I Met the Master

I had walked life's way with an easy tread,
Had followed where comforts and pleasures led.
Until one day in a quiet place
I met the Master face to face.

With station and rank and wealth for my goal,
Much thought for my body but none for my soul,
I had entered to win in life's mad race,
When I met the Master face to face.

I met Him and knew Him and blushed to see
That His eyes full of sorrow were fixed on me;
And I faltered and fell at His feet that day,
While my castles melted and vanished away.

Melted and vanished and in their place
Naught else did I see but the Master's face.
And I cried aloud, "Oh, make me meet
To follow the steps of Thy wounded feet."

My thought is now for the souls of men,
I have lost my life to find it again,
E'er since one day in a quiet place
I met the Master face to face.

—Anonymous

Evangelize!

Give us a watchword for the hour
A thrilling word, a word of power;
A battle-cry, a flaming breath,
That calls to conquest or to death;
A word to rouse the church from rest,
To heed her Master's high behest,
The call is given: Ye hosts arise,
Our watchword is Evangelize!

The glad evangel now proclaim
Through all the earth in Jesus' name;
This word is ringing through the skies,
Evangelize! Evangelize!
To dying men, a fallen race,
Make known the gift of gospel grace;
The world that now in darkness lies,
Evangelize! Evangelize!

—Henry Crocker

Oh, for a Pentecost!

Oh, for a passionate passion for souls!
  Oh, for a pity that yearns!
Oh, for a love which loves unto death!
  Oh, for a fire that burns!

Oh, for a prayer-power that prevails,
  That pours itself out for the lost;
Victorious prayer in the Conqueror's name,
  Oh, for a Pentecost!

—*Anonymous*

STRENGTH PROMISED

As Thy Days

Deut. 33:25.

So shall it ever be.
'Tis planned by One
Whose thought is all for thee,
That in accord with life's great need
A strength divine shall come,
Supplanting weakness, changing greed,
And making plain the pathway home.
In Holy Writ this truth we see,
That as Thy days—so strength shall be.

The marvel of it all!
What wisdom wrought!
Thy weakness to forestall!
Not in advance this blessing falls,
Nor stored for coming days,
Not to be gathered into stalls
Nor bartered for in devious ways;
'Tis surely thine when need makes plea,
For as Thy days—so strength shall be.

The glory, then, be Thine,
O Master, Lord,
For meeting need of mine.
I would not anxious be, nor fret
When burdens press me sore,
But trudge along contented yet
To trust Thee, Lord, and love Thee more
With stronger faith that 'tis for me—
For as Thy days, Thy strength shall be.
                    —*Grant Colfax Tullar*

TEACHERS

A Teacher's Prayer

Lord, speak to me that I may speak
  In living echoes of thy tone;
As thou hast sought, so let me seek
  Thy erring children lost and lone.

O teach me, Lord, that I may teach
  The precious truths thou dost impart,
And wing my words, that they may reach
  The hidden depths of many a heart.

O fill me with thy fulness, Lord,
  Until my very heart o'erflow
In kindling thought and glowing word
  Thy love to tell, Thy praise to show.
                    —*Frances Ridley Havergal*

THANKSGIVING

Psalm 95: 1-7

Oh come, let us sing unto Jehovah;
Let us make a joyful noise to the rock of our salvation.
Let us come before his presence with thanksgiving;
Let us make a joyful noise unto him with psalms.
For Jehovah is a great God,
And a great King above all gods.
In his hand are the deep places of the earth;
The heights of the mountains are his also.
The sea is his, and he made it;
And his hands formed the dry land.
Oh come, let us worship and bow down;
Let us kneel before Jehovah our Maker:
For he is our God,
And we are the people of his pasture, and the sheep of his
    hand.

—Am. Stand. Ver.

Thanksgiving

For all things beautiful, and good, and true;
For things that seemed not good yet turned to good;
For all the sweet compulsions of Thy will
That chastened, tried, and wrought us to Thy shape;
For things unnumbered that we take of right,
And value first when they are withheld;
For light and air; sweet sense of sound and smell;
For ears to hear the heavenly harmonies;
For eyes to see the unseen in the seen;
For vision of the Worker in the work;
For hearts to apprehend Thee everywhere;—
We thank Thee, Lord.

—John Oxenham

(Used by permission of the Author)

The Blessings That Remain

There are loved ones who are missing
  From the fireside and the feast;
There are faces that have vanished,
  There are voices that have ceased;
But we know they passed forever
  From our mortal grief and pain,
And we thank Thee, O our Father,
  For the blessings that remain.

Thanksgiving, oh, thanksgiving,
  That their love once blessed us here,
That so long they walked beside us,
  Sharing every smile and tear;
For the joy the past has brought us,
  But can never take away,
For the sweet and gracious memories
  Growing dearer every day,

For the faith that keeps us patient
  Looking at the things unseen,
Knowing Spring shall follow Winter
  And the earth again be green,
For the hope of that glad meeting
  Far from mortal grief and pain—
We thank Thee, O our Father,
  For the blessings that remain.
                    —*Annie Johnson Flint*
        (Used by permission of the Author)

Thy Name We Bless and Magnify

Infinite Truth and Might! whose love
Unmeasured ceaseless bounties prove,
Our Guide and Refuge, Guard and Stay,
Our Light by night, our Shade by day—
Before Thine altar, Lord Most High,
Thy Name we bless and magnify.

Because our fainting souls have fed
On heavenly wine and living bread;
Because our ears Thy Voice have heard,
And in our life Thy Life hath stirred—
Before Thine altar, Lord Most High,
Thy Name we bless and magnify.

For all Thy goodness has supplied,
For all Thy wisdom has denied,
For all Thy love away has ta'en
Of what we counted joy or gain—
Before Thine altar, Lord Most High,
Thy Name we bless and magnify.

—John Power, Abr.

Give Thanks

For all that God in mercy sends;
For health and children, home and friends,
For comfort in the time of need,
For every kindly word and deed,
For happy thoughts and holy talk,
For guidance in our daily walk,
  For everything give thanks!

For beauty in this world of ours,
For verdant grass and lovely flowers,
For song of birds, for hum of bees,
For refreshing summer breeze,
For hill and plain, for streams and wood,
For the great ocean's mighty flood,
  For everything give thanks!

For sweet sleep which comes with night,
For the returning morning's light,
For the bright sun that shines on high,
For the stars glittering in the sky,
For these and everything we see,
O Lord, our hearts we lift to Thee.
  For everything give thanks!

—Miss Helen Isabella Tupper

Hymn of Gratitude

Great God of Nations, now to Thee,
  Our hymn of Gratitude we raise;
With humble heart and bending knee
  We offer Thee our song of praise.

Thy name we bless, Almighty God,
  For all the kindness Thou hast shown
To this fair land the Pilgrims trod—
  This land we fondly call our own.

We praise Thee that the Gospel's light
  Through all our land its radiance sheds
Dispels the shade of error's night,
  And heavenly blessings round us spreads.

Great God, preserve us in Thy fear;
  In danger, still our Guardian be;
O spread Thy truth's bright precepts here;
  Let all the people worship Thee.

—Anonymous

We Thank Thee

For all life's beauties and their beauteous growth;
For Nature's laws and Thy rich providence;
For all Thy perfect processes of life;
For the minute perfection of Thy work,
Seen and unseen, in each remotest part;
For faith and works and gentle charity;
For all that makes for quiet in the world;
For all that lifts man from his common rut;
For all that knits the silken bond of peace;
For all that lifts the fringes of the night,
And lights the darkened corners of the earth;
For every broken gate and sundered bar;
For every wide-flung window of the soul;
For that Thou bearest all that Thou hast made—
  We thank Thee, Lord.

For perfect childlike confidence in Thee;
For childlike glimpses of the life to be;
For trust akin to my child's trust in me;
For hearts at rest through confidence in Thee;
For hearts triumphant in perpetual hope;
For hope victorious through past hopes fulfilled;
For mightier hopes, born of the things we know;
For hope of powers increased ten thousand fold;
For faith, born of the things we may not know;
For that last hope of likeness to Thyself—
        With quickened hearts,
        That find Thee everywhere,
        We thank Thee, Lord.
                —John Oxenham, in "Bees in Amber"
                (Used by permission of the Author)

The Most Acceptable Gift

We thank Thee, now, O Father,
    For all things bright and good,
The seedtime and the harvest,
    Our life, our health, our food;
Accept the gifts we offer
    For all Thy love imparts,
And, what Thou most desirest,
    Our humble, thankful hearts.
—Matthius Claudius.   Trans. by J. M. Campbell

Thanksgiving

For the days when nothing happens,
    For the cares that leave no trace,
For the love of little children,
    For each sunny dwelling-place,
For the altars of our fathers,
    And the closets where we pray,
Take, O gracious God and Father,
    Praises this Thanksgiving Day.

For our harvests safe ingathered,
  For our golden store of wheat,
For the bowers and the vinelands,
  For the flowers up-springing sweet,
For our coasts from want protected,
  For each inlet, river, bay,
By the bounty full and flowing,
  Take our praise this joyful day.

For the hours when Heaven is nearest
  And the earth-mood does not cling,
For the very gloom oft broken
  By our looking for the King,
By our thought that He is coming,
  For our courage on the way,
Take, O Friend, unseen, eternal,
  Praises this Thanksgiving Day.
                        —*Margaret E. Sangster*
              (Used by permission of the Author)

Gratitude

For sunlit hours and visions clear,
For all remembered faces dear;
For comrades of a single day
Who sent us stronger on our way;
For friends who shared the year's long road
And bore with us the common load;
For hours that levied heavy tolls,
But brought us nearer to our goals;
For insights won through toil and tears—
We thank the Keeper of our years.
                        —*Clyde McGee*

Giving Thanks

Enter into His gates with thanksgiving,
And into His courts with praise:
Give thanks unto Him, and bless His name.
                —*Psalm 100:4, Am. Stand. Ver.*

TIME

This Day Is Thine

This day is thine, a shining gift from Heaven,
　Gleaned for thy use from treasuries of time,
Given in trust to hold until the even,
　This day is thine, a sacred charge sublime.

This day is thine, to be what thou shalt make it,
　Hidden in self or used in service fine;
When thou shalt bring it back to Him who gave it,
　What will it be, this golden day of thine?

This day is thine, thy yesterdays are finished,
　Soon will the present join the changeless past;
Will its bright hours be greater for thy keeping
　Or by the dreaded rust of waste o'ercast?

This day is thine, there may be no tomorrows,
　This day is thine from dawn till setting sun;
May thou at even, like a worthy steward,
　Hear in thy heart the Master's words, "Well done."

—Verna Whinery

Life

Forenoon and afternoon and night,—
　And day is gone,—
So short a span of time there is
　'Twixt dawn and evensong.

Youth,—Middle life,—Old age,—
　And life is past,—
So live each day that God shall say,
　"Well done!" at last.

—Edward Rowland Sill

TRIALS

The Refiner's Fire

He sat by a fire of seven-fold heat,
  As He watched by the precious ore,
And closer He bent with a searching gaze
  As He heated it more and more.

He knew He had ore that could stand the test,
  And He wanted the finest gold
To mold as a crown for the King to wear,
  Set with gems with a price untold.

So He laid our gold in the burning fire,
  Though we fain would have said Him "Nay,"
And He watched the dross that we had not seen,
  And it melted and passed away.

And the gold grew brighter and yet more bright;
  But our eyes were so dim with tears,
We saw but the fire—not the Master's hand—
  And questioned with anxious fears.

Yet our gold shone out with a richer glow,
  As it mirrored a Form above
That bent o'er the fire, though unseen by us,
  With a look of ineffable love.

Can we think that it pleased His loving heart
  To cause us a moment's pain?
Ah, no! but He saw through the present cross
  The bliss of eternal gain.

So He waited there with a watchful eye,
  With a love that is strong and sure,
And His gold did not suffer a bit more heat
  Than was needed to make it pure.

                                        —*Anonymous*

Wit's End Corner

"At their wits' end, they cry unto the Lord in their trouble, and
He bringeth them out."—Psalm 107:27, 28.

Are you standing at "Wit's End Corner,"
    Christian, with troubled brow?
Are you thinking of what is before you,
    And all you are bearing now?
Does all the world seem against you,
    And you in the battle alone?
Remember—at "Wit's End Corner"
    Is just where God's power is shown.

Are you standing at "Wit's End Corner,"
    Your work before you spread,
All lying begun, unfinished,
    And pressing on heart and head,
Longing for strength to do it,
    Stretching out trembling hands?
Remember—at "Wit's End Corner"
    The Burden-bearer stands.

Are you standing at "Wit's End Corner"?
    Then you're just in the very spot
To learn the wondrous resources
    Of Him who faileth not;
No doubt to a brighter pathway
    Your footsteps will soon be moved.
But only at "Wit's End Corner"
    Is the "God who is able" proved.
                 —*Antoinette Wilson*

Afterwards

Light after darkness, gain after loss,
Strength after weakness, crown after cross;
Sweet after bitter, hope after fears,
Home after wandering, praise after tears.

Sheaves after sowing, sun after rain,
Sight after mystery, peace after pain;
Joy after sorrow, calm after blast,
Rest after weariness, sweet rest at last.

Near after distant, gleam after gloom,
Love after loneliness, life after tomb;
After long agony, rapture of bliss—
Right was the pathway leading to this.
                              —*Frances R. Havergal*

Moment by Moment

Never a trial that He is not there;
Never a burden that He doth not bear;
Never a sorrow that He doth not share,
Moment by moment I'm under His care.

Never a heartache, and never a groan,
Never a tear-drop, and never a moan,
Never a danger but there, on the throne,
Moment by moment, He thinks of his own.

Never a weakness that He doth not feel;
Never a sickness that He cannot heal,
Moment by moment, in woe or in weal,
Jesus, my Saviour, abides with me still.
                              —*Daniel W. Whittle*

Thou Remainest

"Thou, O Lord, remainest forever."—Lam. 5:19.

Thou remainest, Thou the changeless,
   Though all else on earth may change,
Old joys fade, new griefs awaken,
   Old things pass and new are strange.
Strength declines and footsteps falter
   On the dark path we must face;
Thou remainest!   Thou remainest!
   God of glory and of grace.

Thou remainest, Thou our refuge,
  When our hopes are all laid low;
Though our faith in man may weaken,
  Faith in Thee will stronger grow.
Heavy burdens weight our shoulders;
  And the night brings no release;
Thou remainest! Thou remainest!
  God of power and of peace.

Thou remainest, Everlasting,
  When all else shall pass away;
Friends are gone and pleasures fail us,
  And the clouds obscure our way,
Still Thy promise stands unshaken,
  Life and death its truth shall prove;
Thou remainest! Thou remainest!
  God of wisdom and of love.

—Annie Johnson Flint
(Used by permission of the Author)

Revelation

If all my days were summer, could I know
The meaning of my Lord's "made white as snow"?

If all my hours were joyous could I say,
"In His fair land, all tears are wiped away"?

If I were never weary could I keep
Close to my heart, "He gives His lov'd ones sleep"?

Were no graves mine could life eternal seem
Anything to me, but baseless dream?

My winters, my tears and my weariness,
Even my graves reveal His blessedness.

I call them ills, yet at rare times I see
That all is love which brings my Lord to me.

—Warren F. Cook

As Thy Days So Shall Thy Strength Be

God broke the years to hours and days,
That hour by hour
And day by day,
Just going on a little way,
We might be able all along
To keep quite strong.
Should all the weights of life
Be laid across our shoulders,
And the future, rife
With woe and struggle,
Meet us face to face
At just one place,
We could not go;
Our feet would stop. And so
God lays a little on us every day,
And never, I believe, on all the way,
Will burdens bear so deep,
Or pathways lie so steep,
But we can go, if by God's power
We only bear the burden of the hour.

—Georgiana Holmes (George Klingle)

He Giveth More

"He giveth more grace" (Jas. 4:6). "He increaseth strength" (Isa. 40:29). "Mercy unto you, and peace, and love, be multiplied" (Jude 2).

He giveth more grace when the burdens grow greater,
  He sendeth more strength when the labors increase;
To added affliction He addeth His mercy,
  To multiplied trials, His multiplied peace.

When we have exhausted our store of endurance,
  When our strength has failed ere the day is half done,
When we reach the end of our hoarded resources,
  Our Father's full giving is only begun.

His love has no limit, his grace has no measure,
  His power no boundary known unto men;
For out of his infinite riches in Jesus
  He giveth and giveth and giveth again.

                                  —*Annie Johnson Flint*
                  (Used by permission of the Author)

When Thou Passest Through the Waters

Do you feel your heart discouraged as you pass along the
    way?
Does there seem to be more darkness than there is of sunny
    day?
It is hard to learn the lesson, as we pass beneath the rod,
That the sunshine and the shadow serve alike the will of
    God.
But to me there comes a promise, like the promise of the
    bow,
That however deep the waters they shall never overflow.

When the flesh is worn and weary and the spirit is de-
    pressed,
When temptation comes upon you like a storm on ocean's
    breast,
There's a haven ever ready for the tempest-driven bird,
There is shelter for the tempted in the promise of the Word;
For the standard of the Spirit shall be raised against the
    foe,
And however deep the waters they shall never overflow.

When sorrow comes upon you that no other soul can share,
And the burden seems too heavy for the human heart to
    bear,
There is One whose grace can comfort if you'll give Him an
    abode,
There's a Burden-bearer ready if you'll trust Him with your
    load;
For the precious promise reaches to the depth of human
    woe,
That however deep the waters they shall never overflow.

When the sands of life are ebbing and I near dark Jordan's
    shore,
When I see the billows rising and I hear the waters roar,
I'll reach out my hands to Jesus, in His bosom I will hide;
It will only be a moment till I reach the other side.
It is then the fullest meaning of the promise I shall know:
"When thou passest through the waters they shall never
    overflow."

                           —*Henry Crowell*

The Red Sea Place in Your Life

Have you come to the Red Sea place in your life,
    Where, in spite of all you can do,
There is no way out, there is no way back,
    There is no other way but—through?
Then wait on the Lord with a trust serene,
    Till the night of your fear is gone,
He will send the wind, He will heap the floods,
    He says to your soul, "Go on."

And His hand will lead you through—clear through—
    Ere the watery walls roll down,
No foe can reach you, no wave can touch,
    No mightiest sea can drown;
The tossing billows may rear their crests,
    Their foam at your feet may break,
But over their bed you may walk dry shod,
    In a path that your Lord will make.

In the morning watch, 'neath the lifted cloud,
    You shall see but the Lord alone,
Where He leads you on from the place by the sea,
    To the land that you have not known;
And your fears shall pass as your foes have passed,
    You shall be no more afraid;
You shall sing His praise in a better place,
    A place that His hand has made.

                         —*Annie Johnson Flint*
        (Used by permission of the Author)

The School of Sorrow

I sat in the school of sorrow.
　The Master was teaching there,
But my eyes were dim with weeping
　And my heart oppressed with care.

Instead of looking upward,
　And seeing His face divine,
So full of tender compassion
　For weary hearts like mine.

I only thought of my sorrow;
　The cross that before me lay,
The clouds that hung thick about me,
　Darkening the light of day.

So, I could not learn my lesson
　And say, "Thy will be done."
And the Master came not near me;
　And the weary hours went on.

At last, in despair I lifted
　My streaming eyes above;
And I saw the Master watching
　With a look of pitying love.

To the cross before me He pointed,
　And I thought I heard Him say,
"My child, thou must learn thy lesson,
　And do thy task to-day.

"Not now may I tell the reason,
　'Tis enough for thee to know
That I, the Master, am teaching
　And appoint thee all thy woe!"

Then kneeling, the cross I lifted.
　For one glimpse of that face divine
Had given me strength to bear it,
　And say, "Thy will, not mine."

And so I learned my lesson;
   And through the weary years,
His helping hand sustained me,
   And wiped away the tears.

And ever the glorious sunlight
   From the heavenly home streamed down,
Where the school-tasks are all ended,
   And the cross is exchanged for the crown.
                        —Harold Hamilton

I Do Not Ask Thee, Lord

I do not ask Thee, Lord,
   That all my life may be
An easy, smooth and pleasant path—
   'Twould not be good for me.
But, oh, I ask to-day
   That strength and grace be given
To keep me fighting all the way
   That leads to God and heaven!

I do not ask Thee, Lord,
   That tears may never flow,
Or that the world may always smile
   Upon me as I go.
From Thee fell drops of blood,
   A thorn-crown pressed Thy Brow,
Thy suffering brought Thee victory then,
   And Thou canst help me now.

And what if strength should fail,
   And heart more deeply bleed?
Or what if dark and lonely days
   Draw forth the cry of need?
That cry will bring Thee down,
   My needy soul to fill,
And Thou wilt teach my yearning heart
   To know and do Thy will.
                        —Anonymous

The All-Sufficient Christ

I do not ask that God will keep all storms away;
But this I pray; when thunders roar and lightnings play,
He'll shelter me.

Weak though I am, I dread not now the tempter's hour.
My Saviour then will be my shield; I know His power;
He'll strengthen me.

When I must cross the river to that other realm,
No fear I'll know if Christ is near and holds the helm.
He'll pilot me.

Then when I stand before the judge at that white throne—
Guilty? Ah, yes! but bought by Christ; He knows His
    own;
He'll plead for me.

—Bernice W. Lubke

Life's Lessons

I learn, as the years roll onward
    And I leave the past behind,
That much I had counted sorrow
    But proves that God is kind;
That many a flower I had longed for
    Had hidden a thorn of pain,
And many a rugged by-path
    Led to fields of ripened grain.

The clouds that cover the sunshine
    They can not banish the sun;
And the earth shines out the brighter
    When the weary rain is done.
We must stand in the deepest shadow
    To see the clearest light;
And often through wrong's own darkness
    Comes the weary strength of light.

The sweetest rest is at even,
  After a wearisome day,
When the heavy burden of labor
  Has borne from our hearts away;
And those who have never known sorrow
  Can not know the infinite peace
That falls on the troubled spirit
  When it sees at last release.

We must live through the dreary winter
  If we would value the spring;
And the woods must be cold and silent
  Before the robins sing.
The flowers must be buried in darkness
  Before they can bud and bloom,
And the sweetest, warmest sunshine
  Comes after the storm and gloom.

—*Anonymous*

Warp and Woof

Some days, you say, are good days
  And other days are bad;
The dark days make you gloomy
  And the bright days make you glad.
But when you weave the cloth of life
  You must use warp and woof,
And the good days and the bad days make
  Your fabric weatherproof.

The fair days are the long strands
  That the shuttle carries through,
And the drab days are the cross weave
  That keeps the fabric true.
The weaver knows his pattern
  As he works upon life's loom,
When he threads the golden warp of hope
  Against the woof of gloom.

—*Harry Halbisch*

(Used by permission of the Author)

Our Light Afflictions

What are our light afflictions here,
 But blessings in disguise?
They only make for us a home
 Of rest beyond the skies.

What if we oft are weary now,
 With burdens hard to bear?
They only make the crown more bright
 When we that crown shall wear.

O, cast thy every care on Him,
 Thou weary burdened one,
And raise to Heaven the trusting prayer,
 Thy will, not mine, be done.

So, when the toil and care shall cease,
 With Jesus thou'lt be blest:
When, folded in His loving arms,
 The weary are at rest.

—Anonymous

And Yet—

The night is dark—
 How shall I go on?
And yet—off there somewhere
 Will be the dawn.

The path is steep,
 And rough with thorns and stones,
And yet—His hand shall bear me up
 And guide me home.

The storm is wild;
 The waves o'erwhelm my sail;
And yet—the Voice will help
 Me not to fail.

My sight is dim;
   What shall I do—or say?
And yet—He of the pierced palm
   Will point the way.

—*Errol B. Sloan*

Security

Storms come and sorrows come,
   And who are we to murmur?
God's hand holds each bit of strife—
   Whose hand is surer, firmer?

Storms come and sadness comes,
   The winds of heartache quicken;
The clouds of doubt are all about,
   Fear's lightning makes them thicken!

Storms come and terrors come,
   Our frail beliefs are shaken;
But—in God's hand we only dream—
   And, in His arms, we waken!

—*Margaret E. Sangster*
(Used by permission of the Author)

I Have Always Found It So

Never mind the clouds which gather
   O'er the pathway as you go,
Each will have a silver lining,
   I have always found it so!

Never lose your faith and courage,
   Tho' the tears may sometimes flow,
There's a joy for ev'ry sorrow,
   I have always found it so.

Ever keep a heart undaunted,
   Trust the One whose love you know,
Christ will be your Guide and Saviour,
   I have always found it so.

Darkest clouds will have a rainbow,
Light upon your path will glow,
God is faithful who has promised,
I have always found it so.

In the sunshine or the shadow,
Anywhere He bids you go,
God is with you as you journey,
I have always found it so.

—*Birdie Bell*

Amen

I cannot say,
Beneath the pressure of life's care to-day,
I joy in these.
But I can say
That I had rather walk this rugged way,
If Him it please.

I cannot feel
That all is well when dark'ning clouds conceal
The shining sun:
But then I know
God lives and loves; and say, since it is so,
"Thy will be done."

I cannot speak
In happy tones; the tear-drops on my cheek
Show I am sad;
But I can speak
Of grace to suffer with submission meek,
Until made glad.

I do not see
Why God should e'en permit some things to be,
When He is love.
But I can see
Though often dimly, through the mystery,
His hand above.

I may not try
To keep the hot tears back; but hush that sigh
"It might have been;"
And try to still
Each rising murmur, and to God's sweet will
Respond—AMEN.

—F. G. Browning

How Can I Smile?

How can I smile when my heart aches
And I am lonely and sad?
Because my Saviour has entered my life
And He can make me glad.

How can I smile when my life seems
A burden too great to bear?
Because my heavenly Father is here,
Awaiting my burdens to share.

How can I smile when I'm bereft
Of much that life holds dear?
Because, though earthly friends forsake,
My heavenly Father is near.

How can I smile when sorrow and pain
Are a part of my daily life?
Because a loving hand is stretched
To help me bear the strife.

How can I smile when home and love
Are taken away from me?
Because my Saviour sends His Spirit
A comfort and guide to be.

And so I can smile from day to day
Though sorrow and loss I bear
For Jesus, my Saviour, knows and loves;
I am ever in His care.

—Florence B. Hodgdon

Jesus Understands

Is the way o'ercast with shadows?
  Does the road seem rough and steep?
Are you weary, heavy laden?
  Do you long for rest and sleep?
Jesus knows! What consolation
  That the Saviour's loving hands
Wait outstretched to help and guide us;
  Troubled soul—he understands.

—*Anonymous*

Convinced by Sorrow

"There is no God," the foolish saith,
  But none, "There is no sorrow."
And nature oft the cry of faith,
  In bitter need will borrow:
Eyes which the preacher could not school,
  By wayside graves are raised,
And lips say "God be pitiful,"
  Who ne'er said, "God be praised."
    Be pitiful, O God!

—*Elizabeth Barrett Browning*

Passing Through

*"When thou passest through the waters, . . . they shall not over-
flow thee. . .—Isa. 43:2.*

"When thou passest through the waters"—
  Deep the waves may be and cold,
But Jehovah is our refuge
  And His promise is our hold;
For the Lord Himself hath said it,
  He, the faithful God and true,—
When thou comest to the waters
  Thou shalt not go down, but through.

Seas of sorrow, seas of trial,
    Bitterest anguish, fiercest pain,
Rolling surges of temptation
    Sweeping over heart and brain,—
They shall never overflow us
    For we know His word is true;
All His waves and all His billows
    He will lead us safely through.

Threatening breakers of destruction,
    Doubt's insidious undertow,
Shall not sink us, shall not drag us
    Out to ocean depths of woe,
For His promise shall sustain us,
    Praise the Lord, whose word is true!
We shall not go down, or under,
    For He saith, "Thou passest through."

                    —*Annie Johnson Flint*
        (Used by permission of the Author)

After

After the darkness and storm
Cometh a radiant light;
After the winds and the rain
Cometh the sunshine bright;
After the gloaming and night
Cometh the glorious dawn;
After the toiling and cares
Cometh the victor's song.

After the turmoil and strife
Cometh a wondrous peace;
After the doubts and the fears
Cometh a sure release;
After the sorrow and tears
Cometh a heavenly strain;
After the prayer and praise
Cometh His blessing again.

                    —*Caroline Grayson*

Some Time We'll Understand

Not now, but in the coming years,
    It may be in the better land,
We'll read the meaning of our tears,
    And there, some time, we'll understand.

CHORUS

Then trust in God through all thy days;
    Fear not! for He doth hold thy hand;
Though dark thy way, still sing and praise:
    Some time, some time, we'll understand.

We'll catch the broken threads again,
    And finish what we here began;
Heaven will the mysteries explain,
    And then, ah, then, we'll understand.

We'll know why clouds instead of sun
    Were over many a cherished plan;
Why song has ceased when scarce begun;
    'Tis there, some time, we'll understand.

Why what we long for most of all
    Eludes so oft our eager hand;
Why hopes are crushed and castles fall,
    Up there, some time, we'll understand.

God knows the way, He holds the key,
    He guides us with unerring hand;
Some time with tearless eyes we'll see;
    Yes, there, up there, we'll understand.
                        —*Maxwell N. Cornelius, D. D.*

May God Give Strength

When Death comes near to grimly claim his toll;
When sorrows surge that nearly whelm the soul;
When looking forward to the heav'nly goal;
    May God give strength.

In days when He shall seem to hide His face;
In trials when you need His richest grace;
In moments when you're weary of the race;
  May God give strength.

To trust His love whatever ill befalls;
To do His will no matter when He calls;
To walk with Him whose friendship never palls;
  May God give strength.

—Peter Van Wynen

The Unfailing One

The little sharp vexations,
  And the briars that catch and fret
Why not take all to the Helper
  Who has never failed us yet.

Tell Him about the heartache
  And tell Him the longings too;
Tell Him the baffled purpose
  When we scarce know what to do.

Then leaving all our weakness
  With the One Divinely strong,
Forget that we bore the burden,
  And carry away the song.

—Phillips Brooks

(Used by permission of E. P. Dutton & Co.)

Guide and Friend

He who hath led will lead
  All through the wilderness;
He who hath fed will feed;
  He who hath blessed will bless;
He who hath heard thy cry,
  Will never close His ear;
He who hath marked thy faintest sigh,
  Will not forget thy tear.
He loveth always, faileth never;
So rest on Him, to-day, forever!

Then trust Him to-day
  As thine unfailing Friend,
And let Him lead thee all the way,
  Who loveth to the end.
And let the morrow rest
  In His beloved hand;
His good is better than our best,
  As we shall understand—
If, trusting Him who faileth never,
We rest on Him, to-day, forever!

—*Anonymous*

TRUST

There Is Never a Day So Dreary

There is never a day so dreary but God can make it bright,
And unto the soul that trusts Him He giveth songs in the
    night.
There is never a path so hidden but God will lead the way,
If we seek for the Spirit's guidance, and patiently wait and
    pray.

There is never a cross so heavy but the nail-scarred hands
    are there,
Outstretched in tender compassion, the burden to help us
    bear.
There is never a heart so broken but the loving Lord can
    heal,
For the Lord that was pierced on Calvary doth still for His
    loved ones feel.

There is never a life so darkened, so hopeless and unblest,
But may be filled with the light of God, and enter His
    promised rest.
There is never a sin or sorrow, there is never a care or loss,
But that we may bring to Jesus, and leave at the foot of the
    cross.

—*Lilla M. Alexander*

Try the Uplook

When the outlook is dark, try the uplook.
　These words hold a message of cheer;
Be glad while repeating them over,
　And smile when the shadows appear.
Above and beyond stands the Master;
　He sees what we do for His sake.
He never will fail nor forsake us;
　He knoweth the way that we take.

When the outlook is dark, try the uplook—
　The outlook of faith and good cheer;
The love of the Father surrounds us,
　He knows when the shadows are near.
Be brave, then, and keep the eyes lifted,
　And smile on the dreariest day.
His smile will glow in the darkness;
　His light will illumine the way.

—Anonymous

Quiet from Fear of Evil

"Thou wilt keep him in perfect peace, whose mind is stayed on Thee: Because he trusteth in Thee."—Isa. 26:3.

Quiet from fear of evil,
　Dwelling with Christ my King,
Resting beneath His shadow,
　Gladly my heart shall sing.

Quiet from fear of evil,
　He with His peace endows;
Nothing can touch His children
　But what His hand allows.

Quiet from fear of evil,
　There on the throne above,
High above all the nations,
　Sitteth the King we love.

Quiet from fear of evil,
    Trusting, of Him I sing;
Jesus the world's great Victor,
    Jesus our glorious King.

—*S. C. M'K.*

Leave It With Him

Yes, leave it with Him; the lilies all do,
        And they grow;
They grow in the rain, and they grow in the dew—
        Yes, they grow;
They grow in the darkness, all hid in the night,
They grow in the sunshine, revealed by the light—
        Still they grow.

They ask not your planting, they need not your care
        As they grow.
Dropped down in the valley, the field—anywhere—
        Yet, they grow.
They grow in their beauty, arrayed in pure white;
They grow, clothed in glory, by heaven's own light—
        Sweetly they grow.

The grasses are clothed and the ravens are fed
        From His store;
But you who are loved and guarded and led,
        How much more
Will He clothe you, and feed you, and give you His care!
Then, leave it with Him; he has, everywhere,
        Ample store.

Yes, leave it with Him; 'tis more dear to His heart,
        You will know,
Than the lilies that bloom or the flowers that start
        'Neath the snow.
Whatever you need, if you ask it in prayer,
You can leave it with Him, for you are His care—
        You, you know.

—*Anonymous*

A Hymn of Trust

"In quietness and in confidence shall be your strength."—Isaiah
30:15.

In quietness and confidence
My strength shall ever be!
No weariness shall overcome
The soul that's stayed on Thee.
Though trials sore and hardships come
My strength He shall renew;
His presence shall envelop me—
No ill shall e'er pass through.

My case into His hands I've given,
He knoweth all my need;
And He who notes the sparrow's fall
Shall still provide and lead.
Though sudden sorrow pierce my heart,
Though storm-clouds rise and thunders roll,
In quietness and confidence
Shall be my strength of soul.

Though friends may fail, the world be dark,
I know for me He cares,
And as a Father pitieth
In all my grief He shares.
And so, whatever may betide,
Or whether weal or woe,
In quietness and confidence
Shall be the strength I know.

—*Nettie M. Sargent*

Psalm 37: 1-7

Trust in the Lord· So shalt thou dwell
Within the land, and daily tell
How He thy soul doth ever feed,
And well supply thine every need.

Delight thyself in Him alway;
In shine or storm; by night, by day;
Thine heart's desires He will fulfill,
And give the strength to do His will.

Commit to Him thine every way,
And He will guide thee day by day;
Thy righteousness shine as the light,
Thy judgment be as noonday bright.

Rest in the Lord, and wait for Him;
E'en though thy path be often dim.
Fret not, O child of God, thine heart,
For Jesus Christ will peace impart.
—*Charles Frederic Sheldon, D. D.*

Safe In His Keeping

(Psalm 4:8)

When night is come, and all around is still,
And gentle sleep my weary eyes would close:
O heart of mine, think not of boding ill,
But rest in God for calm and safe repose.

O heart of mine, still all thy trembling fear!
For He, whose eyes are never closed in sleep,
Is watching o'er thee, gently bending near,
To guard from evil and thy soul to keep.

"In peace will I both lay me down and sleep,"
For in the safety of the Lord I dwell;
His arm of love my trembling soul doth keep,
His presence whispers me that all is well.

And I shall wake to see the morning light
In this fair world, or on the other side—
No matter where; I know it will be bright,
For in His keeping I shall still abide.
—*Edgar Cooper Mason*
(Used by permission of the Author)

Day by Day

I heard a voice at evening softly say:
"Bear not thy yesterday into tomorrow,
  Nor load this week with last week's load of sorrow;
Lift all thy burdens as they come, nor try
  To weight the present with the by and by.
One step and then another, take thy way—
        Live day by day.

"Live day by day.
Though the autumn leaves are withering round thy way,
  Walk in the sunshine. It is all for thee.
Push straight ahead as long as thou canst see.
Dread not the winter where thou mayst go;
  But when it comes, be thankful for the snow.
Onward and upward. Look and smile and pray—
        Live day by day.

"Live day by day.
The path before thee doth not lead astray.
  Do the next duty. It must surely be
The Christ is in the one that's close to thee.
Onward, still onward, with a sunny smile,
  Till step by step shall end in mile by mile.
'I'll do my best,' unto my conscience say—
        Live day by day.

"Live day by day.
Why are thou bending toward the backward way?
  One summit and another thou shall mount.
Why stop at every round the space to count
The past mistakes if thou must still remember?
  Watch not the ashes of the dying ember.
Kindle thy hope. Put all thy fears away—
        Live day by day."

                —*Julia Harris May*

Hitherto Hath the Lord Helped

*"Then Samuel took a stone, ... and called the name of it
Ebenezer, saying, 'Hitherto hath the Lord helped us.' "—I. Sam. 7:12.
"Jesus Christ the same yesterday, and today, and forever."—Heb.
13:8.*

O thou of little faith,
God has not failed thee yet!
When all looks dark and gloomy,
Thou dost so soon forget—

Forget that He *has* led thee,
And gently cleared thy way;
On clouds has poured His sunshine,
And turned thy night to day.

And if He's helped thee hitherto,
He will not fail thee *now*;
How it must wound His loving heart
To see thy anxious brow!

O doubt not any longer,
To Him commit thy way,
Whom in the past thou trusted,
And is "the same to-day."

—Anonymous

Faith, Hope and Love

*"And now abideth faith, hope, charity, these three; but the great-
est of these is charity."—I. Cor. 13:13.*

FAITH sees beyond the grave,
A home of rest;
And whispers in the gloom,
"God's will is best."

HOPE, like a shining star,
Brightens life's way;
Gives courage to the faint,
From day to day.

LOVE, greatest gift of all,
  Calms ev'ry fear;
Makes all our burdens light,
  Brings Heaven near.

—By an Invalid

He Leadeth Me

In pastures green? Not always; sometimes He
Who knoweth best, in kindness leadeth me
In weary ways, where heavy shadows be—

Out of the sunshine warm and soft and bright,
Out of the sunshine into darkest night;
I oft would faint with sorrow and affright—

Only for this—I know He holds my hand,
So whether in the green or desert land.
I trust, although I may not understand.

And by still waters? No, not always so;
Ofttimes the heavy tempests round me blow,
And o'er my soul the waves and billows go.

But when the storms beat loudest, and I cry
Aloud for help, the Master standeth by,
And whispers to my soul, "Lo, it is I."

Above the tempest wild I hear Him say,
"Beyond this darkness lies the perfect day,
In every path of thine I lead the way."

So, whether on the hill-tops high and fair
I dwell, or in the sunless valleys where
The shadows lie—what matter? He is there.

And more than this; where'er the pathway lead
He gives to me no helpless, broken reed,
But His own hand, sufficient for my need.

So where He leads me I can safely go;
And in the blest hereafter I shall know
Why in His wisdom He hath led me so.

—H. H. Barry

Leave the Miracle to Him

"Whatsoever he saith unto you, do it."—John 2:5.

"Whatsoe'er He bids you—do it!"
  Though you may not understand;
Yield to Him complete obedience,
  Then you'll see His mighty hand.
"Fill the waterpots with water,"
  Fill them to the very brim;
He will honor all your trusting,—
  Leave the miracle to Him!

Bind your Isaac to the altar,
  Bind him there with many a cord;
Oh, my brother, do not falter,
  Can't you fully trust your Lord?
He it is who watches o'er you,
  Though your faith may oft be dim;
He will bring new life to Isaac,—
  Leave the miracle to Him!

See them march around the city,
  Scarce a sound from day to day;
Scoffers from the walls deride them—
  "Jericho can stand such play!"
But the Lord's time cometh swiftly,
  Then they shout out with a vim;
Look, the walls are tottering, falling,—
  Leave the miracle to Him!

Face to face with hosts of Midian,
  Gideon's men are sifted out;
Forth they go, these chosen heroes,
  With no sword, the foe to rout.
Do you wonder if the vict'ry
  Can be gained by band so slim?
See! Jehovah's sword is gleaming,—
  Leave the miracle to Him!

Watch that scene on plains of Dura;
  See that Hebrew martyr band
Firmly standing for Jehovah,
  Trusting in His hidden hand.
"He is mighty to deliver"
  From the power of death so grim;
Fiery furnace cannot harm them,—
  Leave the miracle to Him!

Bring to Christ your loaves and fishes,
  Though they be both few and small;
He will use the weakest vessels,—
  Give to Him your little all.
Do you ask how many thousands
  Can be fed with food so slim?
Listen to the Master's blessing,—
  Leave the miracle to Him!

Oh, ye Christians, learn the lesson!
  Are you struggling all the way?
Cease your trying, change to trusting,
  Then you'll triumph every day!
"Whatso'er He bids you—do it!"
  Fill the waterpots to brim;
But, remember, 'tis His battle,—
  Leave the miracle to Him!

Christian worker, looking forward
  To the ripened harvest field,
Does the task seem great before you?
  Think how rich will be the yield!
Bravely enter with your Master,
  Though the prospect may seem dim;
Preach the Word with holy fervor,—
  Leave the miracle to Him!

—*Thomas H. Allan*

Out In the Fields With God

The little cares that fretted me
I lost them yesterday,
Among the fields above the sea,
Among the winds at play;
Among the lowing of the herds,
The rustling of the trees;
Among the singing of the birds,
The humming of the bees.

The foolish fears of what might happen,
I cast them all away
Among the clover-scented grass,
Among the new-mown hay;
Among the husking of the corn,
Where drowsy poppies nod,
Where ill thoughts die and good are born—
Out in the fields with God!

—Elizabeth Barrett Browning

We See Jesus

"But we see Jesus."—Heb. 2:9.

I don't look back: God knows the fruitless efforts,
    The wasted hours the sinning, the regrets;
I leave them all with Him Who blots the record,
    And mercifully forgives, and then forgets.

I don't look forward, God sees all the future,
    The road that, short or long, will lead me home,
And He will face with me its every trial,
    And bear for me the burdens that may come.

I don't look round me: then would fears assail me,
    So wild the tumult of earth's restless seas;
So dark the world, so filled with woe and evil,
    So vain the hope of comfort or of ease.

I don't look in; for then am I most wretched;
   Myself has naught on which to stay my trust;
Nothing I see save failures and short-comings,
   And weak endeavors crumbling into dust.

But I look up—into the face of Jesus,
   For there my heart can rest, my fears are stilled;
And there is joy, and love, and light for darkness,
   And perfect peace, and every hope fulfilled.

—Annie Johnson Flint
(Used by permission of the Author)

Overheard In an Orchard

Said the Robin to the Sparrow:
   "I should really like to know
Why these anxious human beings
   Rush about and worry so?"

Said the Sparrow to the Robin:
   "Friend, I think that it must be
That they have no heavenly Father
   Such as cares for you and me."

—Elizabeth Cheney

The Serenity of Faith

Hear, O Lord, my loud cry,
   And graciously answer me.
My heart hath said unto Thee,
   "Thy face, O Lord, I seek."

Hide not Thy face from me,
   Reject not Thy servant in anger:
   For Thou hast been my help.
Abandon me not, nor forsake me,
   O God of my salvation:
For father and mother have left me;
   But the Lord will take me up.

Teach me Thy way, O Lord:
Lead me in an even path,
Because of mine enemies.
Give me not up, O Lord,
Unto the rage of my foes;
For against me have risen false witnesses,
Breathing our cruelty.

Firm is the faith I cherish,
That I, in the land of the living,
Shall yet see the goodness of God.
Let thy heart be courageous and strong
And wait on the Lord.
—Psalm 27:7-14; McFadyen's Translation

God's Plans

If we could push ajar the gates of life,
And stand within, and all God's workings see,
We could interpret all this doubt and strife,
And for each mystery could find a key.
But not today. Then be content, poor heart!
God's plans, like lilies pure and white, unfold:
We must not tear the close-shut leaves apart—
Time will reveal the calyxes of gold.
—Mary Riley Smith

A Question

If I really, really trust Him,
Shall I ever fret?
If I really do expect Him,
Can I e'er forget?
If by faith I really see Him,
Shall I doubt His aid?
If I really, really love Him,
Can I be afraid?
—Anonymous

Trus' an' Smile

Honey, trus' der Lawd a bit, an' doan fohgit to smile!
Ain' no use a-frettin' an' a-mou'nin' all de while—
S'pose de rain does peppah down, an' s'pose de skies am
    gray;
Shuah de Good Lawd ain' gwine let it always be dat way!
He's jest' sendin' trials for to put yuh to de tes';
Dat's His way ob tryin' out de ones He lubs de bes'.
Doan' yuh 'member Daniel in de fierce ol' lion's den?
He jes' smile an' trus' his Lawd, an' out he come again!
When de Hebrew chillun in de fiery furnace lit
Dey jes' smile an' trus' de Lawd, an' didn' burn a bit!
When you'ah jes plum scared to def an' doan' know what
    to do,
Dat's de time de helpin' han' reach down an' guide yuh
    froo!
Shuah He ain' a-fixing to fohgit yuh is His chile—
Honey, trus' de Lawd a bit, an' doan' fohgit to smile!
—*B. Y. Williams*

More of Thee

Not what I am, O Lord, but what Thou art,
    That, that alone can be my soul's true rest;
Thy love, not mine, bids fear and doubt depart,
    And stills the tempest of my throbbing heart.

Thy name is Love, I hear it from yon cross;
    Thy name is Love, I hear it from yon tomb:
All meaner love is perishable dross,
    But this shall light me through times thickest gloom.

Girt with the love of God on every side,
    Breathing that love as heaven's own healing air,
I work or wait, still following my Guide,
    Braving each foe, escaping every snare.

'Tis what I know of Thee, my Lord, my God,
    That fills my soul with peace, my lips with song;
Thou are my health, my joy, my staff and rod;
    Leaning on Thee, in weariness I am strong.

More of Thyself, O show me hour by hour;
    More of Thy glory, O my God and Lord;
More of Thyself, in all Thy grace and power;
    More of Thy love and truth, Incarnate Word.
                                —*Dr. Horatius Bonar*

Sleep Sweet

Sleep sweet within thy quiet room,
    O thou, whoe'er thou art,
And let no mournful yesterday
    Disturb thy peaceful heart;
Nor let to-morrow scare thy rest
    With dreams of coming ill;
Thy Maker is thy changeless friend,
    Whose love surrounds thee still.
Forget thyself and all the world,
    Put out each feverish light;
The stars are watching overhead.
    Sleep sweet; good night, good night.
                                —*Ellen M. Gates*

A Trust-Song

When the day is stormy, and no sun shines through
    Clouds that gather o'er us, shutting out God's blue,
Think 'tis shining somewhere, and take heart of grace;
    Let the joy of trusting take the sunshine's place.

If God send the shadow as he sends the sun,
    There's a purpose in it, so—His will be done!
Trust Him, never doubting; trust Him, come what may;
    And grow glad in trusting all along the way.

Let us, then, in storm-time, feel that God knows best,
  He's behind the tempest, trust Him for the rest!
So in faith unfalt'ring, let the moments run,
  Trusting in the shadow, trusting in the sun.

Trust and let the sunshine of God's love shine through
  Every overhanging cloud that darkens over you.
                              —*Eben E. Rexford*

Be Still

"Be still and know that I am God!"
Be still? O Soul, how can it be?
When dangers threaten as a flood—
Temptations trouble as the sea!

"Be still and know that I am God!"
Be still? O Saviour, I would flee
When suffer I thy chastening rod.
In silence shall I stand with Thee?

"Be still and know that I am God!"
Be still? O Master, cares oppress!
Life's tasks are heavy as I plod
Heart-sick and faint with weariness.

"Be still and know that I am God!"
Be still! What peace, what solace thine.
Thy rest, my rest, by grace bestowed;
Thy yoke and thy light burden, mine.
                      —*William Ward Ayer*
          (Used by permission of the Author)

The Time to Trust

When nothing whereon to lean remains,
  When strongholds crumble to dust;
When nothing is sure but that God still reigns,
  That is just the time to trust.
                              —*Anonymous*

The Divine Lover

Jesus, Lover of my soul,
    Let me to Thy bosom fly,
While the nearer waters roll,
    While the tempest still is high;
Hide me, O my Saviour, hide,
    Till the storm of life is past;
Safe into the haven guide,
    Oh, receive my soul at last.

Other refuge have I none,
    Hangs my helpless soul on Thee;
Leave, oh, leave me not alone,
    Still support and comfort me;
All my trust on Thee is stayed,
    All my help from Thee I bring;
Cover my defenseless head
    With the shadow of Thy wing.

Thou, O Christ, art all I want;
    More than all in Thee I find;
Raise the fallen, cheer the faint,
    Heal the sick, and lead the blind.
Just and holy is Thy name,
    I am all unrighteousness;
Vile, and full of sin I am,
    Thou art full of truth and grace.

Plenteous grace with Thee is found
    Grace to cover all my sin;
Let the healing streams abound,
    Make me, keep me, pure within.
Thou of life the Fountain art,
    Freely let me take of Thee:
Spring Thou up within my heart,
    Rise to all eternity.

                                    —*Charles Wesley*

Life and Love

Yet Love will dream and Faith will trust,
Since He who knows our need is just,
That somewhere, somehow, meet we must.
Alas for him who never sees
The stars shine through his cypress-trees;
Who hopeless lays his dead away,
Nor looks to see the breaking day
Across the mournful marbles play;
Who hath not learned, in hours of faith,
The truth to flesh and sense unknown,
That life is ever lord of death,
And love can never lose its own!

—J. G. Whittier

"Trust In God!"

Courage brother! do not stumble,
Though thy path be dark as night,
There's a star to guide the humble,
Trust in God, and do the right.

Though the road be long and dreary,
And its ending out of sight,
Foot it bravely—strong or weary,
Trust in God, and do the right.

—Norman Macleod

Refuge

'Mid all the ceaseless rush of life
  We dwell in Thine eternal calm;
For every pain the world may bring
  We find in Thee unfailing balm;
Nor fears of future years disturb
  The souls who in Thy goodness rest;
Nor change, nor loss, nor sorrow's pang,
  If all by Thy dear hand are blest.

In faith we sail an unknown sea
  Serene, by Thee, our Pilot, led;
Deep unto deep is calling Thee,
  But under all Thine arms are spread;
Though wide and far the way we take,
  We move within Thy circling love;
We sink, and, lo! Thine arms upraise;
  We rise, and Thou dost smile above.
                    —*Mabel E. McCartney*

WILL OF GOD

Thy Will Be Done

Thy will, O God, is best,
By Thee the victory's won,
In Thy strong will we find our rest,
Thy will, O God, be done.

Thy will, O God, is strong,
Resist Thy power can none,
Thy throne is raised above all wrong,
Thy will, O God, be done.

Thy will, O God, is law,
Thy word through worlds hath run,
Teach us to say with holy awe,
Thy will, O God, be done.

Thy will, O God, is love,
Thou art our shield and sun,
In earth below, in heaven above,
Thy will, O God, be done.

Thy will, O God, is life,
Thy life and ours is one,
Be Thou our master in the strife,
Until Thy will is done.
                    —*Hugh Thomson Kerr, D. D., LL. D.*
(Used by permission of the Author)

His Will Be Done

"His will be done," we say with sighs and trembling.
  Expecting trial, bitter loss and tears;
And then how doth He answer us with blessings
  In sweet rebuking of our faithless fears.

God's will is peace and plenty and the power
  To be and have the best that He can give,
A mind to serve Him and a heart to love Him,
  The faith to die with and the strength to live.

It means for us all good, all grace, all glory,
  His kingdom coming and on earth begun,
Why should we fear to say: "His will—His righteous,
  His tender, loving, joyous will—be done"?
                              —*Annie Johnson Flint*

Trust and Obedience

Thou knowest what is best;
  And who but Thee, O God, hath power to know?
In Thy great will my trusting heart shall rest;
  Beneath that will my humbled head shall bow.

Then what Thou pleasest, send;
  To order all my destiny is Thine,
With Thee, in all Thy purposes to blend,
  For unity of heart, let that be mine.

No questions will I ask,
  Do what Thou wilt, my Father and my God,
Obedience is my consecrated task,
  Though it should lead me where Thy martyrs trod.

Alike, all pleases well,
  Since living faith has made it understood,
Within the shadowy folds of sorrow dwell
  The seeds of life and everlasting good.
                              —*Anonymous*

God's Will

I asked the Master for a motto sweet,
Some rule of life by which to guide my feet
   I asked and paused—
He answered soft and low,
"God's will to know,
God's will to know."

"Will knowledge then suffice?" I cried,
But ere the question into silence died,
   The answer came—
"This remember too—
God's will to do,
God's will to do."

Once more I asked, "Is there nothing more to tell?"
And once again the answer softly fell,
   "Yea, this one thing,
All other things above—
God's will to love,
God's will to love."

            —Charles E. Guthrie

God's Will Is Best

Thy Will is best for me,
Whate'er it bringeth me;
Of loss or gain, of joy or pain,
Thy Will is best for me.

            —Anonymous

God's Will

God's Will in me
Is Life and Immortality.

God's Will in me
Is Truth and Good and Purity.

God's Will in me
Is Faith and Hope and Charity.

God's Will in me
Is Health and sweet Simplicity.

God's Will in me
Is one symphonic Harmony.

When one with Thee, my life shall be
Attuned to gladsome Melody.

—Alice Nevin

Consecration

My Jesus, as Thou wilt!
  O may Thy will be mine;
Into Thy hand of love
  I would my all resign.
Through sorrow, or through joy,
  Conduct me as Thine own;
And help me still to say,
  My Lord, Thy will be done.

My Jesus, as Thou wilt;
  Though seen through many a tear,
Let not my star of hope
  Grow dim or disappear.
Since Thou on earth hast wept
  And sorrowed oft alone,
If I must weep with Thee,
  My Lord, Thy will be done.

My Jesus, as Thou wilt!
  All shall be well for me;
Each changing future scene
  I gladly trust with Thee.
Straight to my home above
  I travel calmly on,
And sing, in life or death,
  My Lord, Thy will be done.

—Benjamin Schmolck

WORKING FOR GOD

Service

O Master, let me walk with thee
In lowly paths of service free;
Tell me thy secret; help me bear
The strain of toil, the fret of care.

Help me the slow of heart to move
By some clear, winning word of love;
Teach me the wayward feet to stay,
And guide them in the homeward way.

Teach me Thy patience; still with Thee
In closer, dearer company,
In work that keeps faith sweet and strong,
In trust that triumphs over wrong;

In hope that sends a shining ray
Far down the future's broadening way;
In peace that only Thou canst give,—
With Thee, O Master, let me live.

—Washington Gladden

Your Mission

(This was President Lincoln's favorite song, one which he encored repeatedly when sung at a Sunday School Convention in Washington, in 1864.)

If you can not on the ocean
  Sail among the swiftest fleet,
Rocking on the highest billows,
  Laughing at the storms you meet,
You can stand among the sailors
  Anchored yet within the bay;
You can lend a hand to help them
  As they launch their boat away.

If you are too weak to journey
　Up the mountains, steep and high,
You can stand within the valley
　While the multitudes go by,
You can chant in happy measure
　As they slowly pass along;
Though they may forget the singer
　They will not forget the song.

If you have not gold and silver,
　Ever ready to command;
If you can not toward the needy
　Reach an ever helping hand,
You can reach the afflicted,
　O'er the erring you can weep;
You can be a true disciple,
　Sitting at the Saviour's feet.

If you can not in the harvest
　Garner up the richest sheave,
Many a grain, both ripe and golden,
　With the careless reapers leave;
Go and glean among the briers
　Growing rank against the wall,
For it may be that the shadows
　Hide the heaviest wheat of all.

If you can not in the conflict
　Prove yourself a soldier true;
If where fire and smoke are thickest
　There's no work for you to do,
When the battlefield is silent
　You can go with careful tread—
You can bear away the wounded,
　You can cover up the dead.

Do not, then, stand idly waiting
　For some greater work to do;
Fortune is a lazy goddess,
　She will never come to you.

Go and toil in My vineyard,
Do not fear to do or dare;
If you want a field of labor,
You can find it anywhere.

—*Ellen M. Gates*

For the Master's Use

The Master stood in His garden
Among the lilies fair,
Which His own hand had planted
And trained with tenderest care.

He looked at their snowy blossoms,
And marked with observant eye
That His flowers were sadly drooping,
For their leaves were parched and dry.

"My lilies need to be watered,"
The heavenly Master said;
"Wherein shall I draw it for them,
And raise each drooping head?"

Close to His feet on the pathway,
Empty, and frail, and small,
An earthen vessel was lying,
Which seemed of no use at all.

But the Master saw, and raised it
From the dust in which it lay,
And smiled as He gently whispered:
"This shall do my work to-day.

"It is but an earthen vessel,
But it lay so close to me;
It is small, but it is empty,
And that is all it needs to be."

So to the fountain He took it,
And filled it to the brim;
How glad was the earthen vessel
To be of some use to Him!

He poured forth the living water
  Over His lilies fair,
Until the vessel was empty,
  And again He filled it there.

He watered the drooping lilies
  Until they revived again.
And the Master saw, with pleasure,
  That His labor was not in vain.

His own hand had drawn the water
  Which refreshed the thirsty flowers,
But He used the earthen vessel
  To convey the living showers.

And to itself it whispered,
  As He laid it aside once more.
"Still will I lie in His pathway,
  Just where I did before.

"Close would I keep to the Master,
  Empty would I remain,
And some day He may use me
  To water His flowers again."

—Anonymous

My Daily Prayer

If I can do some good today,
If I can serve along life's way,
If I can something helpful say,
  Lord, show me how.

If I can right a human wrong,
If I can help to make one strong,
If I can cheer with smile or song,
  Lord, show me how.

If I can aid one in distress,
If I can make a burden less,
If I can spread more happiness,
  Lord, show me how.

If I can do a kindly deed,
If I can help some one in need,
If I can sow a fruitful seed,
  Lord, show me how.

If I can feed a hungry heart,
If I can give a better start,
If I can fill a nobler part,
  Lord, show me how.
                        —*Grenville Kleiser*

While the Days Are Going By

There are lonely hearts to cherish
  While the days are going by;
There are weary souls who perish,
  While the days are going by;
If a smile we can renew,
As our journey we pursue,
Oh, the good that we may do,
  While the days are going by.

There's no time for idle scorning,
  While the days are going by;
Let your face be like the morning,
  While the days are going by;
Oh, the world is full of sighs,
Full of sad and weeping eyes;
Help your fallen brothers rise,
  While the days are going by.

All the loving links that bind us
  While the days are going by;
One by one we leave behind us,
  While the days are going by;
But the seeds of good we sow,
Both in shade and shine will grow.
And will keep our hearts aglow,
  While the days are going by.
                        —*George Cooper*

Pray - Give - Go

Three things the Master hath to do
  And we who serve Him here below
And long to see His Kingdom come
  May Pray or Give or Go.

He needs them all—the Open Hand,
  The Willing Feet, the Praying Heart—
To work together, and to weave
  A three-fold cord that shall not part.

Nor shall the giver count his gift
  As greater than the worker's deed,
Nor he in turn his service boast
  Above the prayers that voice the need.

Not all can Go; not all can Give,
  To speed the message on its way,
But young or old, or rich or poor,
  Or strong or weak—we all can Pray:

Pray that the gold-filled hands may Give
  To arm the others for the fray;
That those who hear the call may Go,
  And pray—that other hearts may Pray!

—*Annie Johnson Flint*

(Used by permission of the Author)

The Weaver

I sat at my loom in silence,
Facing the western sun;
The warp was rough and tangled
And the threads unevenly run.
Impatiently I pulled at the fibers—
They snapped and flew from my hand;
Weary and faint and sore hearted
I gathered the broken strands.

I had beautiful colors to work with—
White, blue like heaven above,
And tangled in all the meshes
Were the golden threads of love;
But the colors were dulled by my handling,
The pattern was faded and gray,
That once to my eager seeming
Shone fairer than flowers of May.

But alas, not the half of my pattern
Was finished at set of sun;
What should I say to the Master—
When I heard him call, "Is it done?"
I threw down my shuttle in sorrow
(I had worked through the livelong day)
And I lay down to slumber in darkness,
Too weary even to pray.

In my dreams a vision of splendor,
An angel, smiling faced,
With gentle and tender finger
The work of the weavers traced,
He stooped with a benediction
O'er the loom of my neighbor near,
For the threads were smooth and even
And the pattern perfect and clear.

Then I waited in fear and trembling.
As he stood by my tangled skein,
For the look of reproach—and pity
That I knew would add to my pain,
Instead, with a thoughtful aspect,
He turned his gaze upon me,
And I knew that he saw the fair picture
Of my work as I hoped it would be.

And with touch divine of his finger
He traced my faint copy anew,
Transforming the clouded colors,
And letting the pattern shine true,

And I knew in that moment of waiting,
While his look pierced my very soul through,
I was judged not so much by my doing
As by what I had striven to do.

—Anonymous

INDEX TO SUBJECTS

235

INDEX OF AUTHORS

INDEX TO FIRST LINES

Printed in the United States of America